Problem Solving Workbook

with Reading Strategies

Harcourt Brace & Company

Orlando • Atlanta • Austin • Boston • San Francisco • Chicago • Dallas • New York • Toronto • London

http://www.hbschool.com

CONTENTS

Using Mental Math

Write the correct answer.

1. Write the missing number to complete the equation.

$$3 + 8 = \underline{\ ?\ } + 4$$

_____

2. Write the missing number to complete the equation.

$$9 - \underline{\ ?\ } = 2 + 4$$

_____

3. At its first stop, the school bus picks up 5 children. At the next stop, it picks up 6 children. At the final stop, it picks up 4 children. How many children does it pick up in all?

_____

4. Nellie puts 6 quarts of canned tomatoes and 8 quarts of tomato sauce in a large pot. Then she pours the mix into a 12-quart bowl until it is full. How much mix does she have left in the pot?

_____

Choose the letter of the correct answer.

5. Which number will complete the equation?

$$15 - 8 = 4 + \underline{\ ?\ }$$

A 3 **B** 5
C 6 **D** 2

7. Ernie says, "I am thinking of a number between 1 and 100. It's an even number. Its digits add up to 12. It doesn't have a 4 in it." What number is Ernie thinking of?

A 39 **B** 48
C 66 **D** Not Here

6. Which equation can you complete using the number 7?

F $2 + 6 = \underline{\ ?\ } - 3$

G $5 + \underline{\ ?\ } = 14 - 2$

H $12 - \underline{\ ?\ } = 6 + 0$

J $9 + 3 = 18 - \underline{\ ?\ }$

8. **Write About It** Explain the method you used to solve Problem 7.

_____

_____

_____

_____

_____

Adding Three or More Addends

Write the correct answer.

1. Write the perimeter of the figure.

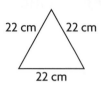

22 cm   22 cm

22 cm

_____

2. Write the sum.

$$\begin{array}{r} 53 \\ 29 \\ 18 \\ + \ 40 \\ \hline \end{array}$$

_____

3. On Tuesday 4 inches of snow fell. Another 3 inches fell on Wednesday, and 8 inches fell on Saturday. How much snow fell in all on the three days?

_____

4. Byron had 18 newspapers. He delivered 5 on Fair Way and 7 on May Road. Then he picked up 6 newspapers before going to Main Street. How many newspapers does he have now?

_____

Choose the letter of the correct answer.

5. Chester's pickup truck can carry 1,500 pounds of pumpkins. Each pumpkin weighs more than 100 pounds. What is the greatest number of pumpkins the truck carry at one time?

A 12   B 14
C 15   D Not Here

6. In a video game, a frog is at the bottom of a well that is 22 feet deep. With each jump, he jumps up 3 feet and slides 2 feet back down. How many jumps will he need to get out of the well?

F 15   G 18
H 21   J 24

7. **Write About It** Explain how you chose your answer for Problem 5.

_____

_____

Observing Patterns

It is helpful to observe patterns. Noticing a pattern can help you solve some problems. Read the following problem. Notice what happens to one measurement as another measurement changes.

Ron has 56 feet of rope to mark off a square area for his garden. He is trying to figure out the length of each side of the garden. He tries 10 feet for the east side and 18 feet for the north side, then 11 feet for the east side and 17 feet for the north side, and then 12 feet for the east side and 16 feet for the north side. He continues in this way until he finds the measurement of each side of the square. What should be the length of each side of the garden?

1. Continue the pattern to complete the table. Find the next two sets of measurements.

East Side	North Side
10 feet	18 feet
11 feet	17 feet
12 feet	16 feet

2. Solve the problem. _____

_____

3. Describe the strategy you used. _____

_____

_____

Observe a pattern. Continue the pattern to solve the problem.

4. Luis has 60 feet of fencing to make a square pen for his pet pig. He tries three sets of measurements: 11 feet by 19 feet, 12 feet by 18 feet, and 13 feet by 17 feet. What should be the length of each side of the pen?

_____

5. Betsy has 64 inches of ribbon to make a border for a square wall hanging. She tries 20 inches by 12 inches, 19 inches by 13 inches, and 18 inches by 14 inches. What should be the length of each side of the border?

_____

Estimating Sums and Differences

Write the correct answer.

1. Round $76.38 to the nearest ten cents.

2. Estimate the difference by rounding to the nearest hundred.
   536 − 390

3. Ann wants to put a border along one edge of a ceiling. The ceiling edge is 20 feet long. She has pieces of border that measure 3 feet, 6 feet, 4 feet, and 5 feet. Does she have enough border?

4. Mr. Lee needs to put molding along the edge of a ceiling. The room is a rectangle 14 feet long and 12 feet wide. How many feet of molding does he need?

Choose the letter of the correct answer.

5. At two years old, a child is about one-half as tall as he or she will be as an adult. Bobbie is two years old and is 34 in. tall. About how tall will she probably be as an adult?

   A About 34 in.   B About 78 in.
   C About 68 in.   D About 80 in.

6. Ted is playing a game on a checkerboard. He moves his piece forward 4 squares, left 3 squares, back 2 squares, and right 3 squares. How many squares does he have to move to be back where he started?

   F 0   G 1
   H 2   J Not Here

7. Which number is the most reasonable estimate of the sum?

   136 + 785 + 205 = _?_

   A 1,000   B 1,100
   C 1,400   D 900

8. Which number rounds to 700 when it is rounded to the nearest ten?

   F 783   G 694
   H 708   J 704

9. **Write About It** Describe the method you used to solve Problem 6.

_____

_____

Adding and Subtracting with Money

Write the correct answer.

1. Write the sum.

   $8.03
   + $9.19

   _____

2. Write the difference.

   $19.54
   − 11.68

   _____

3. Zelda buys four items that cost $3.89, $4.59, $6.89, and $3.99. Will a $20 bill be enough to pay for all of them?

   _____

4. Katie wants to find all of the numbers that round to 70 when rounded to the nearest ten. She writes down 68 and 71. How many others are there?

   _____

Choose the letter of the correct answer.

5. Which subtraction problem has a difference of $8.86?

   A $10.00 − $8.86
   B $10.00 − $2.14
   C $10.00 − $3.14
   D $10.00 − $1.14

6. $13.54 + $12.97 = __?__

   F $26.51
   G $25.51
   H $25.41
   K $26.41

7. This number is less than 80. The sum of its digits is 15. The difference between its digits is 1. Which number is it?

   A 77   **B** 69
   C 78   **D** 96

8. Pete drives 200 miles each day. After 8 days he has completed one-half of his trip. How far will Pete's trip be altogether?

   F 1,600 mi   **G** 3,200 mi
   H 6,400 mi   **J** 800 mi

9. **Write About It** Explain how adding or subtracting money is like adding or subtracting whole numbers.

   _____

   _____

   _____

Adding and Subtracting Larger Numbers

Write the correct answer.

1. The perimeter of the figure is 1,095 yards. Find the missing length.

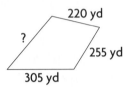

220 yd
?
255 yd
305 yd

_____

2. The perimeter of the figure is 558 feet. Find the missing length.

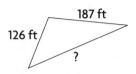

187 ft
126 ft
?

_____

3. Edgar pays for an $18.36 purchase with a $20.00 bill. How much change should he receive?

_____

4. The three sides of a triangle are 63 feet, 48 feet, and 95 feet. Estimate to the nearest ten feet the perimeter of the triangle.

_____

ɔose the letter of the correct answer.

5. A cornfield has 6 sides. Five of the sides measure 380 meters, 276 meters, 290 meters, 312 meters, and 344 meters. The perimeter of the field is 1,907 meters. What is the measure of the sixth side?

   A 315 m   B 225 m
   C 380 m   D 305 m

6. A square park measures 824 feet on each side. The town wants to put an iron fence around the park. Which measure shows how many feet of fence the town will need?

   F 824 ft   G 1,648 ft
   H 3,296 ft   J 4,000 ft

7. Marcie drinks 2 bottles of water every day. Every Friday, she buys all her water for the week. What is the least number of bottles Marcie must have on Sunday morning?

   A 20   B 18
   C 14   D 10

8. The odometer on Xavier's car reads 2,352 miles. During the day, Xavier drove 62 miles to visit his sister, 42 miles to work, and 28 miles to visit the doctor. What did the odometer read at the start of the day?

   F 2,352   G 2,484
   H 2,220   J 2,232

9. **Write About It** Explain the method you used to solve Problem 7.

_____

_____

More Subtracting Across Zeros

Write the correct answer.

1. Write the difference.

$$13{,}002$$
$$- 4{,}273$$

_____

2. Write the difference.

$$7{,}000$$
$$- 5{,}405$$

_____

3. The perimeter of a classroom is 124 feet. Two of the walls are 28 feet long. A third wall is 34 feet long. How long is the fourth wall?

_____

4. Charlie buys two books that cost $6.99 and $4.99. The tax on the books is $0.65. How much does Charlie have to pay?

_____

Choose the letter of the correct answer.

5. $77{,}052 - 24{,}917 = \underline{?}$

A 52,135   **B** 53,945
C 51,135   **D** 53,135

6. Which subtraction problem has a difference of 3,111?

F $8{,}900 - 5{,}799$ **G** $8{,}900 - 5{,}789$
H $5{,}000 - 2{,}890$ **J** $3{,}111 - 3{,}111$

7. Magda went to bed at 9:30 P.M. She woke up at 1:30 A.M. and read for 1 hour and 30 minutes. Then she fell asleep and slept until 6:30 A.M. How many hours of sleep did Magda get?

A 8 hr   **B** 8 hr 30 min

C 9 hr   **D** 7 hr 30 min

8. In 1996, Central City got a total of 28 inches of snow. In 1997, it got a total of 30 inches of snow. The 1998 total was between the 1996 total and the 1997 total. How much snow did Central City get during the three years?

F About 29 in.   **G** About 58 in.
H About 60 in.   **J** About 87 in.

9. Write About It Explain how you solved Problem 7.

_____

_____

_____

Choosing Relevant Information

Sometimes a word problem contains information that may *not* help you solve the problem. You must decide which information is **relevant**, or needed to solve the problem. Read the following problem.

VOCABULARY
relevant
not relevant

> Donna was putting away library books from the book cart. She put 7 books on the science shelves. She put 12 books on the mystery shelves. She put away 4 mystery books that she found on a table. She put 8 books on the history shelves. There were 14 books left on the cart. How many books were on the cart to begin with?

1. Read each fact from the problem. Write whether the fact is *relevant* or *not relevant* to solve the problem.

   a. Donna was putting away library books from the book cart. _____

   b. She put 7 books on the science shelves. _____

   c. She put 12 books on the mystery shelves. _____

   d. She put away 4 mystery books that she found on a table. _____

   e. She put 8 books on the history shelves. _____

   f. There were 14 books left on the cart. _____

2. Solve the problem. _____

3. Describe the strategy you used. _____

   _____

Draw a line through the information that is not relevant. Solve.

4. Lauren hung 7 pictures of dogs in her bedroom. She hung 9 pictures of cats. Lauren has 2 cats and 1 dog. She hung 4 pictures of horses. She had 5 more pictures to hang. How many animal pictures did Lauren have?

   _____

5. Benny bought 14 stamps to add to his stamp collection. His brother gave him 9 stamps. He gave his brother $5.00. Benny now has 68 stamps in his collection. How many stamps did he have to begin with?

   _____

Estimating Sums and Differences

Write the correct answer.

1. Round the number 3,850 to the nearest thousand.

_____

2. Round each addend to the nearest thousand to estimate the sum.

$$\begin{array}{r} 3,480 \\ 2,552 \\ + 7,082 \\ \hline \end{array}$$

_____

3. Richard wrote 800 pages of a novel. Then he took 231 of those pages out of the novel. How many pages were left in the novel?

_____

4. A squirrel ran all the way around the sides of a house trying to get in. The rectangular house was 50 feet long and 24 feet wide. How far did the squirrel run?

_____

Choose the letter of the correct answer.

5. Which number rounds to 3,000 when rounded to the nearest thousand?

A 2,500   B 2,400
C 3,500   D 3,600

6. Which is an estimate of the difference when rounded to the nearest hundred?

$$\begin{array}{r} 6,820 \\ - 2,364 \\ \hline \end{array}$$

F 4,000   G 4,400
H 4,500   J 5,000

7. Frank read 13 magazines during the first week on vacation. He read another 15 during the second week. There were 8 magazines Frank had not read. How many magazines did he take on vacation?

A 36   B 48
C 8   D Not Here

8. Write About It Explain how to estimate a sum by rounding.

_____

_____

_____

_____

_____

_____

Name _____

Choosing the Operation

Write the correct answer.

For Problems 1–4, tell whether you should *add* or *subtract* to solve.
Then solve the problem.

1. Carrie biked 300 miles across the state. Then she biked 220 miles to the ocean. How far did she bike in all?

_____

2. Roger biked 740 miles during another trip. George biked 890 miles during his trip. How much farther did George bike?

_____

3. The class builds a model of the Pentagon building. Each of the model's five sides is 16 inches long. What is the perimeter of the model?

_____

4. Ellen buys two new tires. The total cost is $76.70. She pays with a $100 bill. Estimate how much change she should get back.

_____

Choose the letter of the correct answer.

5. $54,000 - 7,832$ ___?___

A 46,168   B 47,278
C 46,278   D 47,168

6. Which is the most reasonable estimate of the difference $6,094 - 3,604$?

F 2,000   G 2,500
H 3,500   J 1,500

7. Melanie's math teacher wrote this pattern of numbers on the board: 100, 94, 86, 76, 64. What is the next number in the pattern?

A 58   B 56
C 52   D 50

8. Tom counts the stairs as he climbs to his apartment twice a day. He counts 16 steps, then 13 steps, then 12 steps, and then 12 steps. How many steps does he climb each day?

F 53   G 16
H 29   J 106

9. **Write About It** Describe the pattern you saw in the numbers in Problem 7.

_____

_____

What Questions Can Multiplication Answer?

Write the correct answer.

1. Doug bowls 3 times each week. How many times does he bowl during 4 weeks?

   _____

2. Newton eats 2 apples each day. How many apples does he eat in 7 days?

   _____

3. Yolanda drove 3,941 miles in August. She drove 2,412 miles in September. Estimate how many miles she drove in all.

   _____

   _____

4. Janice earned $32.58 at the tag sale. Carla earned $39.19. How much more money did Carla earn than Janice?

   _____

   _____

Choose the letter of the correct answer.

5. A classroom has 6 rows of students with 5 students in each row. What is the total number of students in the classroom?

   A 24   **B** 11   **C** 36   **D** 30

6. Sang has written a book of poetry. The book has 4 sections. Each section has 7 poems. How many poems are there in the book?

   F 7   **G** 24   **H** 28   **J** 11

7. Thomas shovels snow for three of his neighbors. They each pay him $10. He also walks dogs for two other neighbors. They each pay him $12. How much more money does he make from shoveling snow?

   A $10   **B** $15
   C $6   **D** $4

8. A researcher surveys people in a town. Nine of the people were born in the town. Eight moved to the town from out of state. One person moved to the town from another country. How many people did the researcher survey?

   F 34   **G** 18
   H 10   **J** Not Here

9. **Write About It** Explain the steps you took to solve Problem 7.

   _____

   _____

   _____

Multiplication Properties

Write the correct answer.

1. Use a multiplication property to help you find the product.

$$8 \times 1$$

_____

2. Use a multiplication property to help you find the product.

$$0 \times 7$$

_____

3. On Monday Aaron saw 119 geese. On Tuesday he saw 210. On Wednesday he saw 184. Estimate the total number of geese he saw during the three days.

_____

_____

4. Vlad is collecting money for the Salvation Army. He collects $41.18 on Wednesday and $76.42 on Saturday. How much more money does he collect on Saturday?

_____

Choose the letter of the correct answer.

5. Charles Lindbergh set a record in 1927 by flying alone from the U.S. to Paris. Two pilots set a record in 1986 by flying around the world without stopping. How many years passed between these two flights?

   A 60 years   **B** 49 years
   C 59 years   **D** 70 years

6. In the 1950s, there were 21 successful space launches. In the 1960s, there were 854 successful launches. How many successful launches took place during the 1950s and 1960s?

   F 875   **G** 833
   H 885   **J** Not Here

7. Which property will help you find the product?

$$310 \times 0$$

   A Property of One
   B Zero Property
   C Order Property
   D Not Here

8. Which property will help you find the product?

$$1 \times 97$$

   F Property of One
   G Zero Property
   H Order Property
   J Not Here

9. **Write About It** Use your own words to explain the Order Property of Multiplication.

_____

_____

Multiplying Three Factors

Write the correct answer.

1. Show two ways to group the factors using parentheses.

   $6 \times 5 \times 7$

   _____

2. Write the product.

   $9 \times (4 \times 3)$

   _____

3. Mark buys 3 packs of baseball cards. Each pack holds 5 cards. How many cards does he buy?

   _____

4. Vicki needs 500 points to win a game. In the first round she gets 187 points. In the second round she gets 212 points. In the third round she gets 236 points. Estimate whether she has enough points to win.

   _____

Choose the letter of the correct answer.

5. Which multiplication problem has a product of 64?

   A $2 \times (6 \times 8)$ **B** $(2 \times 4) \times 8$
   C $(2 \times 6) \times 6$ **D** $2 \times (3 \times 4)$

6. Which number is the product of $8 \times (3 \times 2)$?

   F 88   **G** 48
   H 26   **J** 19

7. Will drives for three days. Every day he drives twice as many miles as the day before. After three days he has driven a total of 630 miles. How many miles did he drive on the first day?

   A 630 mi   **B** 315 mi
   C 90 mi   **D** 158 mi

8. There are 8 fruit bars in a box. There are 6 boxes in each case. A store orders 5 cases. Which expression could you use to find the total number of fruit bars the store orders?

   F $8 \times 3 \times 5$ **G** $(5 \times 6) \times 5$
   H $8 \times (6 \times 5)$ **J** Not Here

9. **Write About It** Explain how you got your answer in Problem 7.

   _____

   _____

   _____

Name _____

Visualizing/Using Pictures

Drawing a picture can help you **visualize**, or see, what a problem is describing. As you read the problem, draw a picture of what is being described. Read the following problem.

> At the pet store, the puppies are in 3 rows of 2 cages each. There are 4 puppies in each cage. How many puppies are there in all?

---

1. Draw a picture to show what is being described in each part of the problem.

	Visualize/Use a Picture
At the pet store, the puppies are in 3 rows of 2 cages each.	
There are 4 puppies in each cage.	

2. Solve the problem. _____

3. Describe the strategy you used. _____

_____

Draw a picture to visualize and solve each problem.

4. The cat cages at the pet store are in 3 rows of 3. Janice put 3 bowls of cat food in each cage of cats. In all, how many bowls of cat food did she put in the cages?

_____

5. Bob discovered that 2 cats at the pet store had kittens. Each cat had 4 kittens. How many paws do the kittens have in all?

_____

Name _____

Choosing the Operation

Write the correct answer.

1. Dorchester has 7 pizza parlors. Easton has 3 pizza parlors. Which operation would you use to find the number of pizza parlors the two cities have altogether?

   _____

2. A farmer is hatching eggs. She has 4 incubators. Each incubator has 8 eggs. Which operation would you use to find how many eggs there are in all?

   _____

3. Harry delivers 4 TVs each work day. He works 5 days each week. How many TVs does he deliver during a 4-week period?

   _____

4. A rock concert attracts 30,000 fans. The hall has only 22,550 seats. How many fans will not get in to the concert?

   _____

Choose the letter of the correct answer.

5. Craig lives on the 6th floor. Barb lives on the 9th floor. The number of floors between them is _?_. Which number sentence would you use to solve this problem?

   A $6 - \underline{?} = 9$ **B** $9 + 6 = \underline{?}$
   C $9 \times 6 = \underline{?}$ **D** $9 - 6 = \underline{?}$

6. Tony climbs the stairs to the 9th floor. Then he climbs up 6 more floors. He ends up on the _?_ floor. Which number sentence would you use to solve this problem?

   F $6 - \underline{?} = 9$ **G** $9 + 6 = \underline{?}$
   H $9 \times 6 = \underline{?}$ **J** $9 - 6 = \underline{?}$

7. Edna's teacher writes these numbers on the board: 1, 4, 9, 16, 25. He tells her that the numbers in this pattern are called square numbers. Which number comes next in the pattern?

   A 34
   B 36
   C 49
   D 50

8. Each soccer team has 5 girls and 4 boys. There are 8 soccer teams. Which operations will give you the total number of players on all of the soccer teams?

   F Multiplication, then subtraction
   G Multiplication, then addition
   H Addition, then multiplication
   J Not Here

9. **Write About It** Explain the rule for the pattern in Problem 7.

_____

_____

What Questions Can Division Answer?

Write the correct answer.

1. There are 20 students in a classroom. The students sit in 4 rows. Each row has the same number of students. How many students are there in each row?

   _____

2. Trent charges $5 each day to walk 1 dog. He walks 4 dogs. He walks them every day for a week. How much money does Trent make for the week?

   _____

3. Five friends share a bag of pretzels. Each friend has 6 pretzels. How many pretzels were in the bag?

   _____

4. A train carries 24 passengers. There are 8 passengers in each car. How many cars are there?

   _____

Choose the letter of the correct answer.

5. Fifteen students go on a class trip. Three students travel in each car. How many cars are there?

   A 2   B 3
   C 4   D 5

6. A triangle has sides that are 14 cm, 15 cm, and 22 cm long. What is the perimeter of the triangle?
   F 41 cm   G 51 cm
   H 4,620 cm   J 7 cm

7. Lars's stamp album has 18 pages. The last page has 8 stamps. All the other pages each have 12 stamps. Which number sentence can you use to find the total number of stamps?

   A $18 \times 8 + 12$
   B $18 \times 12 + 8$
   C $17 \times 12 + 8$
   D $17 \times 8 + 12$

8. The temperature in Ann Arbor one morning is 2°F. One month later, the temperature is 69°F warmer. What is the temperature one month later?

   F 67°F
   G 78°F
   H 73°F
   J Not Here

9. **Write About It** Explain how you use division to solve Problem 1.

   _____

   _____

Connecting Multiplication and Division

Write the correct answer.

1. Write a related multiplication fact.

   $18 \div 3 = 6$

   _____

2. Write the multiplication and division fact family for the numbers 4, 7, and 28.

   _____

   _____

3. Charles wants to plant 35 flowers in 5 flower beds. He decides to plant the same number in each flower bed. How many does he plant in each?

   _____

4. Didi made an $11.87 purchase. She gave the cashier a $20 bill. The cashier gave her $6.13 in change. Did the cashier give her the correct change? Explain.

   _____

Choose the letter of the correct answer.

5. Which multiplication fact could you use to help you find the quotient of $36 \div 9$ __?__

   A $6 \times 6 = 36$ **B** $4 \times 9 = 36$
   C $2 \times 2 = 4$ **D** $3 \times 3 = 9$

6. Dan sells 32 candy bars to 8 houses. Each neighbor buys the same number of candy bars. How many candy bars does each buy?

   F 2   **G** 3
   H 4   **J** 5

7. A car drives around a 4-mile racetrack 16 times. Then it drives another 3 miles and runs out of gas. Which number sentence can you use to find the total number of miles the car drives before it runs out of gas?

   A $16 \div 4 - 3$ **B** $16 \div 4 + 3$
   C $16 \times 4 - 3$ **D** $16 \times 4 + 3$

8. Blaise is playing a bongo drum. He taps the drum with his right hand 3 times, his left hand 1 time, then his right hand 2 times. He repeats this pattern 6 times during a song. How many times does he tap the drum?

   F 16   **G** 25
   H 36   **J** Not Here

9. **Write About It** Explain how you solved Problem 4.

   _____

   _____

Interpreting Answers and Remainders

It is important to understand what **answers** and **remainders** represent in a word problem. Read the following problem.

There will be 48 guests at Joe's dinner party. He wants to put them into groups of 5, 6, or 7 people, with each group at a separate table. How many tables will he need for each way of grouping the guests? In which grouping will there be the same number of guests at each table?

1. Complete the table to show the different possible ways to group the guests.

Total Number of Guests	Number of Guests in Each Group	Number of Groups	Number of Tables Needed
48	5	$48 \div 5 = 9 \, r3$	10

2. Solve the problem. _____

_____

3. Describe the strategy you used. _____

_____

_____

Interpret the answer and remainder in each problem. Solve.

4. Lily has 35 books to place in a bookcase. She can place them in groups of 6 to a shelf in a blue bookcase or in groups of 7 in a red bookcase. How many shelves will she need if she uses the blue bookcase? if she uses the red bookcase?

5. Jake needs 8 boxes for packing books. Boxes come in packages of 2 and in packages of 3. In how many different ways can he buy exactly 8 boxes? Explain.

_____

_____

_____

Division on a Multiplication Table

Write the correct answer.

1. Write the quotient.
$56 \div 8$

_____

2. Write the quotient.
$81 \div 9$

_____

3. Write the multiplication and
division fact family for the
numbers 54, 9, 6.

_____

_____

4. The storeroom has 3 layers of
boxes. Each layer has 3 rows of
boxes. Each row has 8 boxes in it.
How many boxes are there in all?

_____

Choose the letter of the correct answer.

5. There are 72 tickets sold to 9 fans.
Each fan buys the same number of
tickets. How many tickets does
each fan buy?

A 6 **B** 72
C 8 **D** 9

6. There are 63 tickets sold to a
group of fans. Each fan buys 7
tickets. How many fans buy
tickets?

F 6 **G** 63
H 7 **J** 9

7. Myrna's dog starts barking at
10:30 P.M. It does not stop barking
until 1:30 A.M. How many hours
does the dog bark?

A 1 hr **B** 2 hr
C 3 hr **D** 4 hr

8. A wheat field has 5 sides. Each
side has 6 fence posts along it.
How many fence posts are there
around the wheat field?

F 29 **G** 20
H 25 **J** Not Here

9. Write About It Did you have to perform an operation to
solve Problem 6? Explain.

_____

_____

Recording and Practicing Division

Write the correct answer.

1. Write the quotient.

$6\overline{)42}$

_____

2. Write the quotient.

$8\overline{)32}$

_____

3. Dahlia plants 37 trees, Marv plants 41 trees, and Maura plants 48 trees. Estimate the total number of trees planted.

_____

4. Phil buys the 128-ounce bag of cat food for his 2 cats. His cats eat 84 ounces of food. How many ounces of food does Phil have left?

_____

Choose the letter of the correct answer.

5. $63 \div 7$?

A 7   **B** 9   **C** 8   **D** 6

6. Which number is the quotient when you divide $9\overline{)45}$?

F 2   **G** 3   **H** 4   **J** 5

7. Tyrell lives where the streets are numbered. As you drive north in the city, the street numbers get higher. Tyrell drives 42 blocks north from 112th Street to meet a friend. Then they drive 46 blocks south to a park. What street is the park on?

A 112th Street
B 158th Street
C 116th Street
D 108th Street

8. Lydia has been juggling for 2 weeks. She can now juggle 4 hoops at once. A week ago she could juggle only 3 hoops. How many hoops could she juggle before she started practicing?

F Lydia could juggle 6 hoops.
G Lydia could juggle 4 hoops.
H Lydia could juggle 0 hoops.
J Not enough information given.

9. Write About It Explain how you solved Problem 7.

_____

_____

_____

Choosing the Operation

Write the correct answer.

1. A physicist makes a new wire that is 1,000 atoms thick. She has a wire that is 750 atoms thick. How many atoms thicker is the new wire?

_____

2. A large truck spills a crate of nails. The nails give the truck 7 flat tires. The truck still has 9 full tires. How many tires does the truck have in all?

_____

3. Olivia makes fruit baskets for 6 friends. She buys 48 pieces of fruit. Each basket has the same number of pieces of fruit. How many pieces of fruit does Olivia put in each basket?

_____

4. On his first birthday Aaron knows about 25 words. On his second birthday Aaron knows about 1,000 words. About how many more words did Aaron learn by his second birthday?

_____

Choose the letter of the correct answer.

5. Which number is the quotient?
$$64 \div 8$$

   A 8   **B** 6   **C** 5   **D** 9

6. Which number is the quotient?
$$7\overline{)56}$$

   F 6   **G** 7   **H** 8   **J** 9

7. Martha Washington was born in 1732. She married George Washington 27 years later. She died in 1802. How many years passed between her marriage and her death?

   A 43 years   **B** 27 years
   C 70 years   **D** 59 years

8. Carol practiced piano for twice as long as Gregory. Gregory practiced piano 2 hours longer than Wanda. Wanda practiced piano for 4 hours. How long did Carol practice the piano?

   F 6 hr   **G** 8 hr
   H 12 hr   **J** Not Here

9. **Write About It** Explain the method you used to solve Problem 8.

_____

_____

Name _____

LESSON
5.1

How Numbers Are Used

Write the correct answer.

1. Write *cardinal, ordinal,* or *nominal* to describe the 4 in "4 quarts of milk."

_____

2. Write *cardinal, ordinal,* or *nominal* to describe the 7 in "7th-inning stretch."

_____

3. Write *cardinal, ordinal,* or *nominal* to describe the number.

_____

4. Write *cardinal, ordinal,* or *nominal* to describe the number.

_____

Choose the letter of the correct answer.

5. Which month is the third month of the year?

   A March
   B June
   C April
   D May

6. Which sentence uses the number 5 as an ordinal number?

   F John won 5th place.
   G Bob lives at 25 Kings Way.
   H Cal lost 5 pounds.
   J Bette is 5 feet tall.

7. Kevin knows that the flagpole is 80 feet tall. It is about as tall as the building behind it. The building has 8 floors. About how high is each floor?

   A About 8 ft   B About 10 ft
   C About 15 ft   D About 4 ft

8. Sally rides the bus to school and home. On Wednesdays and Fridays, her mother picks her up at school to go to choir practice. How many times does Sally ride the bus each school week?

   F 14   G 10
   H 8   J Not Here

9. **Write About It** Explain how you solved Problem 8.

_____

_____

PS22   PROBLEM SOLVING

Name _____

More About How Numbers Are Used

Write the correct answer.

1. Write the ordered pair that describes where the rose is on the garden map.

   _____

2. Write the name of the flower that is at (5, 5) on the garden map.

   _____

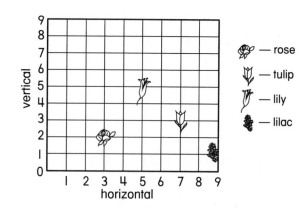

3. Victoria won 2nd place in the talent show. Write *cardinal*, *ordinal*, or *nominal* to describe the number 2 in 2nd place.

   _____

4. Nathan's baseball uniform has the number 9 on it. Write *cardinal*, *ordinal*, or *nominal* to describe this use of the number 9.

   _____

Choose the letter of the correct answer.

5. Which flower is located at (9,1) on the map above?

   A rose   **B** lily

   C lilac   **D** tulip

6. Which ordered pair identifies the tulip on the map above?

   F (2, 4)   **G** (1, 9)

   H (5, 5)   **J** (7, 3)

7. In Leesburg, there is no 1st Street. The street numbering starts with 2nd Street and goes up to 44th Street. How many numbered streets are there?

   A 44   **B** 43

   C 45   **D** 46

8. Vince climbed to the top of three mountains. The mountains were 13,211 feet high, 14,599 feet high, and 10,408 feet high. Which is a reasonable estimate of how many feet Vince climbed in all?

   F 55,000 ft   **G** 38,000 ft

   H 21,000 ft   **J** 28,000 ft

9. **Write About It** Explain why you chose the number you did to solve Problem 8.

   _____

   _____

More About 1,000

Write the correct answer.

1. Write the number of thousands, hundreds, tens, and ones.

7,364

_____

_____

2. "Carlos is a 3rd-generation U.S. citizen." Write *cardinal*, *ordinal*, or *nominal* to describe the number 3.

_____

3. Write the number shown by the base-ten blocks.

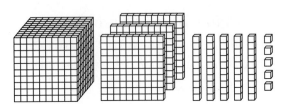

_____

4. Write an ordered pair to describe the location of the hotel.

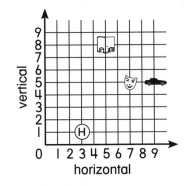

Ⓗ Hospital
🚗 Parking
🎭 Theater
🏨 Hotel

_____

Choose the letter of the correct answer.

5. Which digit tells how many thousands are in 2,349?

   A 2   B 3   C 4   D 9

6. Which digit tells how many hundreds are in 8,042?

   F 8   G 0   H 4   J 2

7. The circus parade travels around the downtown in a square that is 8 blocks on each side. How many blocks does the parade travel?

   A 0   B 8
   C 32   D 64

8. A rooster crows at 5:59 A.M. The sun rises at 6:21 A.M. How many minutes before sunrise does the rooster crow?

   F 21 min   G 20 min
   H 22 min   J Not Here

9. **Write About It** Describe the method you used to solve Problem 8.

_____

_____

Comparing and Contrasting

It is helpful to compare and contrast information in a problem. **Comparing** means finding how things are alike. **Contrasting** means finding how things are different. Read the following problem.

> Bobby and Luanne are playing a board game. Each of them has taken four turns. Bobby has moved 5 spaces forward, 2 back, 6 forward, and 5 back. Luanne has moved 7 spaces forward, 4 back, 3 forward, and 1 back. Who is ahead in the game? How far ahead?

1. List the moves that are alike in the Compare columns, and add. List the different totals in the Contrast columns, and subtract.

Bobby			Luanne		
Compare	**Compare**	**Contrast**	**Compare**	**Compare**	**Contrast**
5 forward	back	forward	forward	back	forward
+ 6 forward	+ back	− back	+ forward	+ back	− back
11 forward	back	spaces	forward	back	spaces

2. Solve the problem. _____

_____

3. Describe the strategy you used. _____

_____

Compare and contrast the facts in each problem. Solve.

4. Robyn and Dale are fishing. They throw back the fish that are too small. Robyn catches 5 fish, throws back 2, catches 4, and throws back 3. Dale catches 6 fish, throws back 4, catches 3, and throws back 2. Who has more fish? How many more?

5. Ken and Jay are trying to get their toy cars as far east as possible by the fourth turn. Ken's car goes 89 inches east, 5 inches west, 90 inches east, and 6 inches west. Jay's goes 87 inches east, 8 inches west, 93 inches east, and 6 inches west. Whose car is farther east at the end? How much farther?

Benchmark Numbers

Write the correct answer.

1. Write an estimate of the number of coins in pile B.

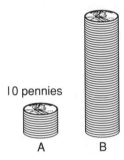

10 pennies

A   B

_____

2. Write an estimate of the number of peanuts in the jar.

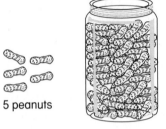

5 peanuts

_____

3. Ned buys a car for $2,860. He must write the amount in words on his check. Write the written form for this number.

_____

4. Janet passes a road sign that says "Steep Hill: Use 2nd Gear." Write *cardinal*, *ordinal*, or *nominal* to describe the 2 in the road sign.

_____

Choose the letter of the correct answer.

5. Each snowball in a snowman is exactly one half as wide as the snowball below it. The snowman is made from 4 snowballs. The top snowball is 6 inches wide. How wide is the bottom snowball?

A 12 in.   B 24 in.
C 48 in.   D 96 in

6. Harry kicked a soccer ball 3 yards farther than Jim. Jim kicked his ball 1 yard less than 20 yards. How far did Harry kick his ball?

F 23 yd   G 22 yd
H 21 yd   J Not Here

7. **Write About It** Explain the strategy you used to solve Problem 5.

_____

_____

_____

Numeration Systems

Write the correct answer.

1.

	Lotus Flower	Scroll	Heel Bone	Stick
Egyptian	⚶	☌	∩		
Standard	1,000	100	10	1

Use the values above to write the Egyptian numeral below, using standard numerals.

⚶⚶⚶ ☌☌ ∩∩∩∩ |||

_____

2. Draw the number 4,405, using Egyptian numerals.

3. Write the number 6,064 in words.

_____

4. Write the number of thousands in 7,952.

_____

Choose the letter of the correct answer.

5. Jaime's math book has 640 pages. Her brother's math book has 421 pages. Which is a reasonable estimate of the total number of pages in both books?

A 1,200   **B** 2,500
C 5,000   **D** 1,000

6. The table in Problem 1 shows Egyptian numerals. How many of those numerals would you have to draw to show the number 9,999?

F 4   **G** 9,999   **H** 36   **J** 9

7. Write About It Explain how you solved Problem 5.

_____

_____

Reading and Writing Numbers

Write the correct answer.

1. Write seven thousand, two hundred four in standard form.

2. Write the number 5,095 in expanded form.

3. Nina spent $8.50 for movie tickets, $3.25 for popcorn, and $1.25 for a drink. How much did Nina spend in all?

4. Write the number that is 100 more than five thousand, four hundred ninety-one.

Choose the letter of the correct answer.

5. Which is the written form for the number 8,407?

   A eight thousand, seventy
   B eight thousand, forty-seven
   C eight hundred forty-seven
   D eight thousand, four hundred seven

6. Which is the standard form for 2,000 + 200 + 2?

   F 2,002
   G 2,202
   H 2,022
   J 2,220

7. Light from the sun takes about 8 minutes to get to Earth. Pam sees the sun peek out from behind a cloud at 10:52 A.M. At what time did the sunlight Pam saw leave the sun?

   A About 2:52 A.M.
   B About 10:46 A.M.
   C About 10:44 A.M.
   D Not Here

8. Samantha deposits two checks at her bank. One check reads "five thousand, seven dollars." The other check reads "four hundred thirty-one dollars." Which number shows the total amount Samantha deposits?

   F $5,431
   G $5,437
   H $5,438
   J Not Here

9. **Write About It** Explain how you solved Problem 8.

Name _____

Mental Math and Place Value

Write the correct answer.

1. Write two other names for the number 3,500.

   _____

   _____

2. Use mental math to find the sum.

   2,300 + 4,600

   _____

3. In radio scripts, numbers are often put in written form. How would the number 2,941 be written in such a radio script?

   _____

   _____

4. About 800 people passed through a tollbooth on Wednesday, about 700 people on Thursday, and 900 people on Friday. About how many people passed through the tollbooth?

   _____

Choose the letter of the correct answer.

5. Which is another name for the number 6,800?

   A 68 hundreds   B 800 ones
   C 600 tens   D Not Here

6. Which mental math problem has a sum of 8,400?

   F 3,200 + 5,200 G 2,400 + 5,000
   H 2,100 + 5,300 J 4,100 + 4,100

7. Mr. T. gets in line at the bank. There are three people ahead of him. Mr. W. has Ms. U in front of him and Mr. V. behind him. Which is the correct order of the bank line?

   A Mr. T., Mr. W., Ms. U., Mr. V.
   B Mr. W., Ms. U., Mr. V., Mr. T.
   C Ms. U., Mr. V., Mr. W., Mr. T.
   D Ms. U., Mr. W., Mr. V., Mr. T.

8. There are 5,280 feet in a mile. Which of the choices below is *not* a correct way of naming this length?

   F 52 hundred, 80 feet
   G 5,000 ft + 200 ft + 80 ft
   H 528 hundred feet
   J Not Here

9. **Write About It** What strategy did you use to solve Problem 7?

   _____

   _____

Using Large Numbers

Write the correct answer.

1. Write the number in standard form.

sixty-eight million, one hundred ninety-two thousand, six hundred

_____

2. Write the period name that should go in the blank.

32,230,039 → 32 million, 230 _?_, 39

_____

3. Frank's book wins two awards. The first award is worth $1,500. The second award is worth $4,000. How much are the two awards worth together?

_____

4. In one week 6,300 people visited a park. Of that number, 2,200 visited on Saturday. How many people visited during the rest of the week?

_____

Choose the letter of the correct answer.

5. Demetrios had 450 stamps. He bought 24 new stamps. Which operation would you use to find out how many stamps he has now?

A addition
B subtraction
C multiplication
D division

6. What number comes after nine million, ninety-nine thousand, ninety-nine?

F ten million
G nine million, one hundred
H nine million, ninety-nine thousand, one hundred
J Not Here

7. Mr. Lester has $8,000 to invest in artwork. He buys a painting for $5,200 and a statue for $1,500. How much money does he have left?

A $2,300   **B** $3,700
C $1,500   **D** $1,300

8. Write About It Explain the strategy you used to solve Problem 7.

_____

_____

_____

_____

Making Predictions

By examining information in a problem, you can often use it to make a prediction. A **prediction** is your best guess based on the information given. Read the following problem.

VOCABULARY
prediction

A newspaper office will move to a larger building in 1999 if the newspaper's circulation increases by 4,000 or more. If the change in circulation is less than 4,000, the office will remain where it is. What do you predict will happen? Explain.

Year	Number of Copies in Circulation	Increase from Previous Year
1994	14,798	—
1995	15,430	632
1996	16,630	1,200
1997	18,935	2,305
1998	22,275	3,340

1. Examine the information in the table. Write what happened to the number of copies in circulation between the given years.

from 1994 to 1995?
from 1995 to 1996?
from 1996 to 1997?
from 1997 to 1998?

2. Solve the problem. _____

_____

3. Describe the strategy you used. _____

_____

Make a prediction based on the information given. Solve.

4. Zephyr Book Company plans to change their book covers if book sales in 1999 are less than in 1998. Do you predict they will change their book covers in 1999? Explain.

Year	Sales
1994	682,371
1995	640,023
1996	521,052
1997	402,056
1998	298,120

_____

_____

_____

Comparing on a Number Line

Write the correct answer.

1. Use the number line to compare.
Write < or >.

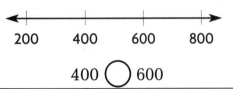

400 ◯ 600
_____

2. Use the number line to compare.
Write < or >.

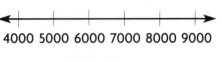

7,000 ◯ 6,000
_____

3. Attendance at the first basketball game was 2,800 people. Attendance at the second game was only 1,100 people. What was the total attendance for both games?

_____

4. Craig and Judy keep records of the jelly beans they eat. Craig has eaten 670 jelly beans. Judy has eaten 570 jelly beans. How many more jelly beans has Craig eaten?

_____

Choose the letter of the correct answer.

5. Willy collected 257 bottles. Leila collected 265 bottles. Who collected more bottles? How many more bottles?

A Willy collected 12 more.
B Willy collected 8 more.
C Leila collected 12 more.
D Leila collected 8 more.

6. The 1790 census counted three million, nine hundred twenty-nine thousand, two hundred fourteen people. Which is this number in standard form?

F 3,929,214
G 392,921,014
H 3,000,929,214
J 392,9214

7. A building is shaped like a pyramid. The first floor has 36 windows. The second floor has 32 windows. The third floor has 28 windows. The pattern continues. The top floor has 4 windows. How many floors are in the building?

A 9   **B** 10   **C** 11   **D** 12

8. Write About It Explain the strategy you used to find your answer to Problem 7.

_____

_____

Comparing Numbers

Write the correct answer.

1. Write the greatest place-value position in which the digits of the two numbers are different in 5,844 and 5,855.

_____

2. Compare the numbers 1,287 and 1,197. Write the comparison, using $<$, $>$, or $=$.

_____

3. A lifeguard estimated that 6,500 people visited a beach on Saturday and 7,300 people visited on Sunday. About how many people visited during the weekend?

_____

4. Mike got three checks for painting houses. He wrote this expression to add the three values: $4,000 + $800 + $90. Write the total in word form.

_____

_____

Choose the letter of the correct answer.

5. Tatiana skates in 5 events at one competition. In the first event, she scores a perfect 10. Her score for each of the other 4 events is between 9 and 10. Which of the following statements can you be sure about?

A Her total is less than 40.
B Her total is between 45 and 49.
C Her total is between 46 and 50.
D Her total is between 47 and 51.

6. Four friends go bowling. Their scores are 126, 128, 136, and 149. Jacob's score is less than Martin's and greater than Becky's. Elise wins the game. Which choice shows their scores?

F E: 149; M: 136; J: 128; B: 126
G E: 149; M: 126; J: 128; B: 136
H E: 149; M: 128; J: 136; B: 126
J Not Here

7. **Write About It** Explain why you made the choice you did in Problem 5.

_____

_____

_____

Analyzing Details

Analyze, or separate, a problem into different parts and then look at one part at a time to help you understand it. Look for important words such as *more*, *fewer*, *at least*, *at most*, *each*, and *exactly* to help you analyze a problem.

Read the following problem.

> Tammy entered 3 events at a horse show. She scored at least 40 on each event. She scored 12 more points on the second event than on the first. She scored 4 fewer points on the third event than on the second. Her three scores totaled 176. What did she score in each event?

---

1. Fill in the table. List the details for each event. Use guess and check to find the scores.

	EVENT 1	EVENT 2	EVENT 3	TOTAL
DETAILS	at least 40			
Points				
Points				
Points				176

2. Solve the problem. _____

3. Describe the strategy you used. _____

_____

Analyze the details in each problem. Solve.

4. David has 11 coins that total $1.22. He has at least 1 penny, 1 nickel, 3 dimes, and 1 quarter. He has, at most, 4 nickels. How many of each coin does he have?

5. The sum of two numbers is exactly 30. Their difference is less than 8 and more than 4. What are the two numbers?

_____

_____   _____

More About Ordering Numbers

Write the correct answer.

1. Write the numbers in order from the greatest to the least.

    3,340; 3,675; 3,430

    _____

2. Write the numbers in order from the least to the greatest.

    5,956; 5,965; 5,696

    _____

3. Brittany threw the javelin 119 ft in Tuesday's meet. In Friday's meet, she threw the javelin 115 ft. During which meet did she throw it farther?

    _____

4. Caleb has two word-processing files on a diskette. The first file is 8,800 bytes. The second file is 6,500 bytes. How much larger is the first file?

    _____

Choose the letter of the correct answer.

5. Which choice shows the numbers ordered from the least to the greatest?

    A 3,248; 3,284; 3,824
    B 3,824; 3,284; 3,248
    C 3,824; 3,248; 3,284
    D 3,284; 3,248; 3,824

6. Which choice shows the numbers ordered from the greatest to the least?

    F 5,092; 5,902; 5,029; 5,920
    G 5,029; 5,092; 5,902; 5,920
    H 5,902; 5,920; 5,092; 5,029
    J 5,920; 5,902; 5,092; 5,029

7. Kate is 3 years older than Heidi. When their ages are added together, they are 21 years old. How old is each girl?

    A Kate: 18 yr; Heidi: 11 yr
    B Kate: 11 yr; Heidi: 10 yr
    C Kate: 13 yr; Heidi: 16 yr
    D Not Here

8. **Write About It** Explain the method you used to order the numbers in Problem 1.

    _____

    _____

    _____

    _____

    _____

Sorting and Comparing

Write the correct answer.

1. Where does the number 87 belong in the Venn diagram?

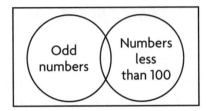

_____

2. Where does the number 153 belong in the Venn diagram?

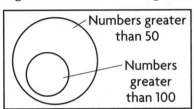

_____

3. Quahog has a population of 3,294. Oyster Bay has a population of 3,249. Crawfish has a population of 3,924. Order the towns from the greatest population to the least.

_____

4. The Jefferson School raises four thousand, eight hundred dollars. The Library Club then donates another one thousand dollars to the school. Write in standard form the total the school has raised.

_____

Choose the letter of the correct answer.

5. $6,400 - 3,100 = \underline{\ ?\ }$

   A 2,000   B 2,300
   C 3,300   D 9,500

6. $2,200 + 5,700 = \underline{\ ?\ }$

   F 7,900   G 3,500
   H 8,900   J 7,500

7. A plumber has a 144-in. length of copper pipe. He cuts off these lengths: 38 in., 42 in., 20 in., 44 in. What length of pipe does he have left?

   A 44 in.
   B 50 in.
   C 60 in.
   D 0 in.

8. A puppy weighed 1 pound. Virgil weighed 84 pounds. A year later, Virgil weighed 101 pounds and the puppy weighed 67 pounds. Who gained more weight? How much more?

   F Virgil; 17 lb more
   G Virgil; 27 lb more
   H The puppy; 49 lb more
   J Not Here

9. **Write About It** In your own words, explain in what ways you can use Venn diagrams.

_____

_____

Telling Time

Write the correct answer.

1. Write *seconds*, *minutes*, *hours*, or *days* to describe the unit you would use to measure the amount of time it takes to read this math problem.

2. Write the time shown on the clock. Include seconds.

3. On Tuesday, Chesterfield had 388 mm of snowfall. On Thursday, it had 412 mm and on Friday, it had 294 mm. Write the days in order from the greatest snowfall to the least snowfall.

4. The town budget of Chesterfield is thirteen million, three hundred ninety-five thousand, eight hundred eleven dollars. Write this amount in standard form.

Choose the letter of the correct answer.

5. The local animal shelter finds homes for 18 cats each month. Which is the most reasonable estimate of the number of cats the shelter finds homes for in 1 year?

   A more than 240 cats
   B less than 240 cats
   C less than 200 cats
   D about 300 cats

6. A digital clock shows 3:42. Which letter shows the same time?

   F 42 minutes before 3
   G 42 minutes past 3
   H 18 minutes before 2
   J 34 minutes before 2

7. **Write About It** Explain why you chose the answer you did for Problem 5.

_____

_____

A.M. and P.M.

Write the correct answer.

1. Use A.M. or P.M. to write the time you leave school.

   _____

2. Write the time 6:00 P.M. as it would appear on a 24-hour clock.

   _____

3. Ned sleeps about 8 hours each night. About how many hours does he sleep in 1 week?

   _____

4. One evening, 3,800 people attend an important town meeting. The town's auditorium can seat only 1,200 people. How many people won't be able to get a seat?

   _____

Choose the letter of the correct answer.

5. A 24-hour clock shows the time 2100. Which letter below shows the same time as it would appear on a 12-hour digital clock?

   A 21:00 P.M.   B 21:00 A.M.
   C 9:00 A.M.   D 9:00 P.M.

6. Which letter shows the time 12 minutes past 3 as it would appear on a digital clock?

   F 12:03   G. 3:21
   H 3:12   J 1:23

7. Tom, Jim, Les, and Marie have a meeting for two o'clock this afternoon. Each one writes down the time for the meeting in a different way. Which way of writing the time is *not* correct?

   A 2:00 P.M.
   B two o'clock this afternoon
   C 1400
   D 2:00 A.M.

8. Ben plays a computer game called *Galaxy*. Every time his spaceship completes a voyage he gets 10 points. How many voyages does he have to complete to get a score of 130 points?

   F 5
   G 10
   H 12
   J 13

9. **Write About It** Describe the method you used to find your answer to Problem 8.

   _____

   _____

Using a Schedule

Write the correct answer.

1. Use the schedule below. Write the elapsed time from the start of the barbecue to the start of the square dance.

DOWN-HOME FESTIVAL	
Event	Start Time
Barbecue	1:00 P.M.
Costume judging	4:30 P.M.
Square dance	6:00 P.M.

_____

2. Use the schedule from Problem 1. Square dancing is scheduled to last for 2 hours, 30 minutes. When will the square dancing end.

_____

3. When Ralph goes to summer camp, bedtime is at 2100. What time is this on a 12-hour clock?

_____

Choose the letter of the correct answer.

4. Each event on the schedule lasts for 45 minutes. At which time will the water-skiing dog event end?

CLYDE'S ANIMAL CIRCUS	
Event	Time
Dancing hippos	10:00 A.M.
Water-skiing dog	11:30 A.M.
Know-it-all parrot	1:15 P.M.

A 11:30 A.M. B 12:00 P.M.
C 12:15 P.M. D 12:15 A.M.

5. Each of 6 vans can hold 10 people. Four of the vans are full. The other 2 vans each have 3 fewer people. How many people are in the vans altogether?

F 60   G 74
H 46   J 54

6. Which number comes next in this pattern: 3, 8, 15, 24, 35?

A 44   B 46
C 48   D 50

7. **Write About It** Describe the rule for the pattern in Problem 6.

_____

_____

_____

Setting a Purpose for Reading

When you read a story, a note, a schedule, or even a word problem, you have a **purpose** for reading it. The purpose may be to gather information, to make a decision, or to be entertained. Read the following problem.

VOCABULARY

purpose

Mr. Baker is reading his daughter's Karate schedule. He needs to find out if he can pick her up from class and be home in time to watch all of a news show that starts at 8:30. The drive home from the class takes 15 minutes. Will he be home in time both days? Explain.

Day	Start Time	Class Length
Monday	6:30	1 hour 30 minutes
Wednesday	7:00	1 hour 30 minutes

---

1. What is Mr. Baker's purpose in reading the schedule? _____

   _____

2. Solve the problem. _____

   _____

3. Describe the strategy you used. _____

   _____

Examine the problem and determine the purpose. Solve.

4. Suppose you want to fly to Chicago. You receive a note from your travel agent telling you that there are three ways you can fly.

   A. You can leave at 1:45 and fly nonstop. The flight will take 5 hours 15 minutes.

   B. You can leave at 1:15 and fly for 2 hours 15 minutes. You will have a 15-minute wait while the plane refuels and then fly 3 hours 30 minutes more.

   C. You can leave at 1:30 and fly for 2 hours 15 minutes. You will have a 15-minute wait while the plane refuels and then fly 2 hours 45 minutes more.

   What is the purpose for the note? What are the arrival times? If you want to arrive as early as possible, which flight should you take?

   _____

   _____

   _____

Elapsed Time on a Calendar

Write the correct answer.

			March			
S	M	T	W	T	F	S
		1	2	3	4	5
6	7	8	9	10	11	12
13	14	15	16	17	18	19
20	21	22	23	24	25	26
27	28	29	30	31		

			April			
S	M	T	W	T	F	S
					1	2
3	4	5	6	7	8	9
10	11	12	13	14	15	16
17	18	19	20	21	22	23
24	25	26	27	28	29	30

			May			
S	M	T	W	T	F	S
1	2	3	4	5	6	7
8	9	10	11	12	13	14
15	16	17	18	19	20	21
22	23	24	25	26	27	28
29	30	31				

1. Use the calendars above. Write the day of the week that is 5 days after March 4.

_____

2. Use the calendars above. Write the date that is exactly 6 weeks before May 18.

_____

3. Nyla starts her workout at 10:45 A.M. She works out for 55 minutes. What time is it when she ends her workout?

_____

4. Chuck's father uses a 24-hour clock. He leaves Chuck a message that he will pick him up at 1600 hours. At what time will Chuck's father be there?

_____

Choose the letter of the correct answer.

5. Vince's birthday is on Leap Day, which is February 29. If the calendars above are from a leap year, on which day of the week was Vince's birthday?

   A Monday   **B** Tuesday
   C Wednesday   **D** Thursday

6. Ella walks around her apartment building looking for her lost dog. She walks around the square building 6 times for a total of 1,920 feet. How long is each side of the building?

   F 60 ft   **G** 80 ft
   H 90 ft   **J** Not Here

7. Use the calendars at the top of the page. Which date is 24 days after March 20?

   A April 14   **B** April 11
   C April 12   **D** April 13

8. Use the calendars at the top of the page. How many days after the first day of April is the last Monday in May?

   F 60 days   **G** 61 days
   H 62 days   **J** 59 days

9. **Write About It** Explain how you solved Problem 6.

_____

_____

Organizing Data in Tables

Write the correct answer.

1. Use the frequency table. How many stars did Chas identify on Thursday night?

STARS I IDENTIFIED EACH NIGHT		
Night	**Stars Identified**	**Cumulative Total of Stars Identified**
Wed.	22	22
Thurs.	28	50
Fri.	46	96

_____

2. Use the frequency table from Problem 1. By the end of Thursday night, how many stars had Chas identified in all?

_____

3. On which night did Chas identify the greatest number of stars?

_____

Choose the letter of the correct answer.

4. Use the frequency table below. On which day did the fewest number of students sign up?

BASKETBALL PRACTICE SIGN-UP		
Day	**Number of Students**	**Total**
Monday	12	12
Tuesday	15	27
Wednesday	9	36
Thursday	41	77

A Monday   **B** Tuesday
C Wednesday   **D** Thursday

5. Use the frequency table from Problem 4. How many students signed up during the first three days?

F 12   **G** 15   **H** 36   **J** 42

6. Joan's car goes 420 miles on a tank of gas. She needs to make a 1,480-mile trip. What is the least number of tanks of gas she will need?

A 1   **B** 2   **C** 3   **D** 4

7. Write About It Explain the difference between the frequency column and the cumulative frequency column on a frequency table.

_____

_____

Classifying and Categorizing

One way to organize information in a problem is to classify and categorize. To **classify** information is to group information that is alike. To **categorize** information is to label the groups, or categories, that you have made by classifying. Read the following problem.

> Jason's school is choosing a student to represent the school at the state capital. The school can choose a student who is 9 years old, 10 years old, 11 years old, or 12 years old. The student can be a boy or a girl. How many possible categories of students can be chosen?

1. Complete the table by classifying and categorizing the information.

2. Solve the problem.

_____

_____

3. Describe the strategy you used.

_____

_____

	Gender
9	boy girl
10	

Classify and categorize the information in each problem. Solve.

4. Duane is making a computer design. He can make a square, rectangle, triangle, or circle. He can print the design in blue, red, or green. How can you classify and categorize the information? How many possible ways can he make the design?

_____

_____

5. Julie is baking a cake. She can bake a chocolate cake, a pound cake, or an angel food cake. She can have vanilla, chocolate, or mint frosting. How can you classify and categorize the information? How many different cakes can she make?

_____

_____

Understanding Surveys

Write the correct answer.

1. Billy took a survey of his classmates. Use his results. Which historical figure did his classmates vote for most often?

FAVORITE HISTORICAL FIGURE OF 4TH GRADERS	
Figure	Votes
Elizabeth Cady Stanton	8
George Washington	11
Abraham Lincoln	9
Martin Luther King, Jr.	12
Thomas Jefferson	5

_____

2. How many of Billy's classmates voted in the survey shown in Problem 1?

_____

3. What are all of the possible outcomes if you toss a dime and a penny one time each?

_____

Choose the letter of the correct answer.

4. Use Billy's survey results from Problem 1. What is the difference between the number of votes for the most and the least popular figures on the list?

   A 4   B 7   C 17   D 20

5. Doug's father opens a 64-ounce carton of orange juice. There is enough juice to pour four full glasses and one half glass. Which is the most reasonable estimate of how much each glass holds?

   F 7 oz   G 12 oz   H 14 oz   J 18 oz

6. **Write About It** Explain the method you used to solve Problem 5.

_____

_____

_____

Name _____

Comparing Graphs

Write the correct answer.

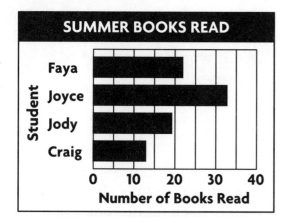

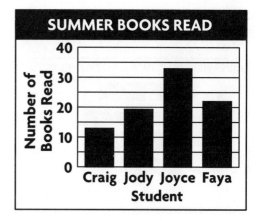

1. What interval is used in the scales of each of the graphs above?

_____

2. Write one way in which the graphs above are different.

_____

_____

3. What are all the possible outcomes if you toss a coin and a number cube numbered 1–6?

_____

_____

4. How many outcomes are possible if you do an experiment with a two-color counter and a spinner with 3 equal sections?

_____

_____

Choose the letter of the correct answer.

5. Use the graphs above. Which student read the fewest books?

  A Faya   B Joyce
  C Jody   D Craig

6. Warren has 6 coins in his pocket. Which of the amounts *cannot* be the total value of the coins?

  F $0.43   G $0.22
  H $0.30   J Not Here

7. **Write About It** Explain how you solved Problem 6.

_____

_____

Name _____

More About Comparing Graphs

Write the correct answer.

1. How could you make the graph below easier to read?

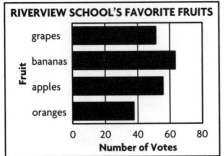

RIVERVIEW SCHOOL'S FAVORITE FRUITS

Fruit: grapes, bananas, apples, oranges

Number of Votes: 0 20 40 60 80

_____

_____

2. Suppose the bars in the graph in Problem 1 were drawn vertically. What would the tallest bar represent?

_____

4. Justin is buying a shirt. He can choose cotton, silk, or rayon fabric. Each fabric comes in a blue, green, gray, or white color. How many shirts are there?

3. How would the graph in Problem 1 change if the interval were 1?

_____

_____

_____

_____

_____

Choose the letter of the correct answer.

5. Gary builds an upside-down pyramid with blocks. He puts 1 block in the first layer, 4 blocks in the second, and 9 blocks in the third. How many blocks would go in the sixth layer?

   A 24   B 30   C 36   D 45

6. In the graph in Problem 1, which fruit received about 40 votes?

   F bananas   G apples
   H grapes   J oranges

7. Which is the best estimate of the total number of votes cast for all four fruits in the graph in Problem 1?

   A 210   B 320   C 380   D 420

8. **Write About It** Describe the rule for the pattern in Problem 5.

_____

_____

Reading a Line Graph

Write the correct answer.

1. Use the graph. What is Horseville's average September temperature?

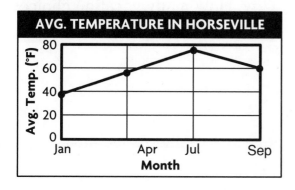

_____

2. Use the survey table. During which two weeks were there the same number of absences?

FEBRUARY ABSENCES AT DIERKER SCHOOL	
Week	**Absences**
1	13
2	15
3	21
4	15

_____

3. Use the graph. During which month is the average Horseville temperature about 55°F?

_____

4. Use the survey table. What was the total number of absences during February?

_____

Choose the letter of the correct answer.

5. Use the graph. Which month had an average temperature of less than 40°F?

   A September   B April
   C July   D January

6. Use the table. Which shows how many more absences there were in Week 3 than in Week 1?

   F 12   G 6   H 8   J 21

7. Jay uses 12 ounces of flour for muffins and 16 ounces for cookies. Then he uses one half of what is left for pancakes, leaving 12 ounces of flour. How much flour did he start with?

   A 52 oz   B 64 oz
   C 16 oz   D 48 oz

8. **Write About It** Describe the method you used to solve Problem 7.

   _____

   _____

   _____

Line Plot

Write the correct answer.

1. Each x on the line plot stands for one student. How many students watched 4 movies?

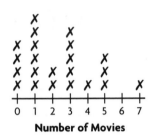

Number of Movies

_____

2. Xenia can go on vacation by bus, train, or plane. She can go to San Francisco, Seattle, or Salt Lake City. How many vacation choices are possible?

_____

3. How many possible outcomes are there if you flip a coin and spin a pointer numbered 1–4?

_____

4. What is the range used in the line plot in Problem 1?

_____

Choose the letter of the correct answer.

5. In the line plot from Problem 1, which number of movies did the greatest number of students see?

   A 0   B 1   C 2   D 3

6. In the line plot from Problem 1, which number of students watched 2 movies?

   F 0   G 1   H 2   J 3

7. Each workday, Valerie needs to put $4.00 into the parking meter when she parks. Parking is $0.50 an hour. The city announces that parking meter costs will rise to $0.60 an hour. How much will it cost Valerie to park on a workday once the new rates are in effect?

   A $5.00   B $0.60
   C $4.80   D $4.00

8. **Write About It** Describe the steps you took to solve Problem 7.

_____

_____

_____

_____

_____

Stem-and-Leaf Plot

Write the correct answer.

1. The stem-and-leaf plot shows the science test scores of Ms. Sitomer's students. What is the median of the scores?

SCIENCE TEST:
MS. SITOMER'S CLASS

Stems	Leaves
7	0 2 2 4 8 9
8	0 0 3 3 4 5 9 9 9
9	0 1 1 2 3 5 8 9

_____

2. Central City voters were asked what they thought was the city's most important issue. Which issue got the most votes?

WHAT IS CENTRAL CITY'S MOST IMPORTANT ISSUE?

Issue	Votes
Crime	32
Land Use	14
Poverty	35
Taxes	29

3. Use the stem-and-leaf plot. What were the highest and lowest scores on the test?

_____

4. Use the survey. Each person surveyed chose one issue. How many people were surveyed?

_____

Choose the letter of the correct answer.

5. Use the stem-and-leaf plot. What is the total number of students in Ms. Sitomer's class who took the science test?

   A 23   B 24   C 26   D 30

7. Ollie makes a pay-phone call that costs $0.75 for the first 3 minutes and $0.15 for each additional minute. Ollie's call costs him $2.10. How long did he talk?

   A 10 min   B 12 min
   C 9 min   D 8 min

6. Use the stem-and-leaf plot. What is the mode of the scores?

   F 85   G 89   H 9   J 80

8. **Write About It** Explain how you found your answer to Problem 7.

   _____

   _____

   _____

   _____

Choosing a Graph

Write the correct answer.

1. Write whether you would use a *line graph, bar graph,* or *stem-and-leaf plot* to show how the price of a gallon of milk changes each month over a year.

_____

2. Write whether you would use a *line graph, bar graph,* or *stem-and-leaf plot* to show the types of pets your classmates have.

_____

3. One fourth-grade class takes a survey to find out the longest bike trip each student has taken. What is the median distance?

_____

4. Use the stem-and-leaf plot. Write the mode of the distances.

_____

LONGEST BIKE TRIPS OF THE FOURTH-GRADE CLASS (in miles)

Stems	Leaves
0	0 0 3 5 8
1	0 0 0 0 0 2 2 5 5 5
2	0 0 5 5 5 5
3	0
4	5

Choose the letter of the correct answer.

5. Which type of display would be the best to display the changes in daily class attendance for the month?

A bar graph
B line graph
C stem-and-leaf plot
D Not Here

6. Leah has a handful of quarters. Tania has 5 times as many coins as Leah. Karl has twice as many coins as Tania. Karl has all dimes. Tania has all nickels. Which friend has the most money?

F Leah   G Tania
H Karl   J Leah and Tania

7. **Write About It** Describe the strategy you used to solve Problem 6.

_____

_____

_____

Name _____

Summarizing

To **summarize** is to state something in a brief way. Knowing how to summarize information is a useful skill. Sometimes using a graph or a plot to display information is a good way to summarize. Read the following problem.

VOCABULARY

summarize

Sue presented this data to her classmates.

NUMBER OF PETS IN STOCK				
Pet	**Dogs**	**Cats**	**Birds**	**Hamsters**
Pedro's Pet Store	5	8	12	10
Animals Galore Pet Store	4	10	14	15

The class wanted to know which pet store generally has more pets in stock. Which pet store does? Explain.

---

1. Complete the graph to summarize the data in the table.

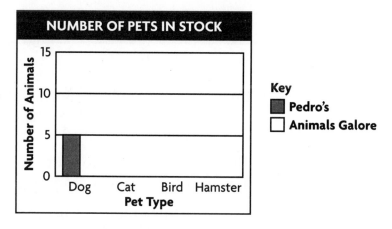

2. Solve the problem. _____

_____

3. Describe the strategy you used. _____

_____

Make a bar graph or line plot to summarize.

4.

WEEKLY WORK SCHEDULE AT SCHOOL LIBRARY				
Student	Alice	Ralph	Trixie	Ed
Hours Worked	4	6	8	5

Certain and Impossible

Write the correct answer.

1. Write the kind of graph or plot you would use to show a family's income for the past 10 years.

_____

2. Write *certain* or *impossible* to describe the chance of rolling a 1, 2, 3, 4, 5, or 6 on a cube numbered 1–6.

_____

3. Write *certain* or *impossible* to describe the chance that tomorrow you will be 36 feet tall.

4. Write the number of players on the baseball team who are 10 years old.

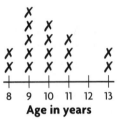

_____

_____

Choose the letter of the correct answer.

5. Which event is certain to happen?

   A Dogs will learn to speak.
   B You will be elected president.
   C You will become a grandparent.
   D Summer will come.

6. Which type of graph or plot would be best to compare the lengths of the 5 longest space walks?

   F line graph   G line plot
   H bar graph   J circle graph

7. Chandra eats lunch at 11:50 A.M. and dinner at 6:25 P.M. How much time passes between the meals?

   A 4 hr 15 min   B 6 hr 35 min
   C 8 hr 15 min   D 3 hr 25 min

8. Dierdra weighed 9 pounds at birth, 18 pounds at six months, and 23 pounds at one year. How much weight did she gain during her first year?

   F 34 lb   G 32 lb
   H 14 lb   J Not Here

9. **Write About It** Describe the method you used to solve Problem 8.

_____

_____

Likely and Unlikely

Write the correct answer.

1. Write *likely* or *unlikely* to describe the chance of landing on blue when using a spinner that has 4 equal sections colored blue, yellow, red, and green.

   _____

2. Write *likely* or *unlikely* to describe the chance that New Mexico will declare independence from the United States.

   _____

3. Write *certain* or *impossible* to describe the chance of rolling an 8 on a cube numbered 1–6.

   _____

4. Which type of graph would be best to show the number of children in each of the houses in your neighborhood?

   _____

Choose the letter of the correct answer.

5. If you spin the pointer 20 times, which number are you likely to spin most often?

   A 5   **B** 10
   C 15   **D** 20

6. Which type of graph would be best to show how much you have grown over the past five years?

   F line graph   **G** line plot
   H bar graph   **J** stem-and-leaf plot

7. Toni is 5 years older than Fran. Fran is twice as old as Ann Marie. Ann Marie is 5 years old. How old is Toni?

   F 15 yr   **G** 8 yr
   H 10 yr   **J** Not Here

8. **Write About It** Describe how you solved Problem 7.

   _____

   _____

   _____

Probability

Write the correct answer.

1. Write a fraction for the probability of spinning an odd number when you spin the pointer below.

_____

2. Write a fraction for the probability of spinning an even number when you spin the pointer from Problem 1.

_____

3. Write *likely* or *unlikely* to describe the chance of spinning a number greater than 4 when you spin the pointer from Problem 1.

_____

4. Write *certain* or *impossible* to describe the chance of spinning a number less than 6 when you spin the pointer in Problem 1.

_____

Choose the letter of the correct answer.

5. Which fraction shows the probability of rolling a 7 when you roll a cube numbered 1–6?

A $\frac{1}{6}$ B $\frac{1}{7}$ C $\frac{7}{6}$ D $\frac{0}{6}$

6. Which fraction shows the probability of rolling an odd number when you roll a cube numbered 1–6?

F $\frac{1}{3}$ G $\frac{2}{6}$ H $\frac{1}{2}$ J $\frac{1}{6}$

7. Violette has an appointment in the city at 3:00 P.M. To get there, she takes a train and then a subway. The subway ride will take 20 minutes. The train ride will take 50 minutes. Which train should she take if she wants to get to her appointment early?

A the 1:55 P.M. B the 1:25 P.M.
C the 2:05 P.M. D the 11:25 P.M.

8. **Write About It** Explain how you chose your answer for Problem 5.

_____

_____

_____

_____

_____

_____

Testing for Fairness

Write the correct answer.

1. Is the spinner fair? Explain why it is or is not.

2. Is the spinner fair? Explain why it is or is not.

_____

_____

_____

_____

3. Write a fraction for the probability of spinning a 5 in Problem 1.

_____

4. Write a fraction for the probability of spinning a square or a triangle in Problem 2.

_____

Choose the letter of the correct answer.

5. What is the median score recorded on the stem-and-leaf plot?

Stem	Leaves
7	5 5 7 8 9
8	1 3 3 5 8 9
9	0 2 2 4 5 9 9 9

Chia's Science Quiz Scores

A 99   B 88   C 83   D 75

6. Wu leaves on a train ride that is scheduled to take 26 hours. The train stalls for 6 hours, and is delayed at one stop another 4 hours. How long does Wu spend on the train?

F 32 hr   G 46 hr
H 36 hr   J Not Here

7. A large carnival spinner is numbered 1–36. Which are you least likely to spin?

A even number B odd number
C multiple of 2 D multiple of 9

8. What is the mode on the stem-and-leaf plot in Problem 5?

F 99   G 88   H 87   J 25

9. **Write About It** Describe the steps you took to solve Problem 6.

_____

_____

Drawing Conclusions

When you examine the evidence and use what you already know to solve a problem, you are **drawing conclusions**. Read the following problem.

> Jamie's dartboard is divided into 6 parts. One half of the board is blue, yellow, and red. The blue and yellow parts are equal. The red part is $\frac{1}{4}$ of the board. The other half of the board is blue, yellow, and green. The blue and yellow parts are equal. Together they are $\frac{1}{4}$ of the entire board. Is the dartboard fair? Explain.

1. Under *Examine the Evidence,* write two more facts that are given. Then write two more helpful facts that you already know.

EXAMINE THE EVIDENCE	USE WHAT YOU ALREADY KNOW
The red part of the first half is $\frac{1}{4}$.	Four fourths make one whole.

2. Solve the problem. _____

3. Describe the strategy you used. _____

_____

Draw conclusions to solve.

4. A rectangular gameboard is divided into 5 parts. The red part is $\frac{1}{4}$ of the rectangle. The blue part is also $\frac{1}{4}$ of the rectangle. The remainder of the board is divided into equal-sized yellow, green, and white parts. Is the gameboard fair? Explain.

_____

_____

_____

5. Allen's spinner is divided into 8 parts. One-fourth of the spinner is white and $\frac{1}{4}$ is black. There are 2 yellow parts and 2 red parts of equal size. Is the spinner fair? Explain.

_____

_____

_____

Name _____

Exploring Geometric Figures

Write the correct answer.

1. Write *one-dimensional, two-dimensional,* or *three-dimensional* to describe the figure.

_____

2. Write *one-dimensional, two-dimensional,* or *three-dimensional* to describe the figure.

_____

3. Write *feet, square feet,* or *cubic feet* to indicate the unit you would use to measure the volume of the box.

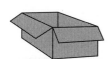

_____

4. Write *feet, square feet,* or *cubic feet* to indicate the unit you would use to measure the length of the rope on the spool.

_____

Choose the letter of the correct answer.

5. Which unit would you use to measure the area of the picture?

A inch   **B** square inch
C cubic inch   **D** degree

6. Which unit would you use to measure the length of the rug?

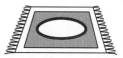

F minute   **G** inch
H cubic inch   **J** square inch

7. Joan is photocopying a picture. She wants to enlarge the picture. Which unit would be used to measure the original?

A feet   **B** cubic feet
C cubic inch   **D** inch

8. Write About It Explain why you chose the answer you did in Problem 5.

_____

_____

_____

_____

Faces of Solid Figures

Write the correct answer.

1. Write the names of the faces and the number of each kind of face on the three-dimensional figure.

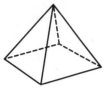

_____

2. Write the names of the faces and the number of each kind of face on the three-dimensional figure.

_____

3. Write *one-dimensional, two-dimensional,* or *three-dimensional* to describe a cube.

_____

4. Write *ft, sq ft,* or *cu ft* to indicate the unit you would use to measure the volume of the figure in Problem 2.

_____

Choose the letter of the correct answer.

5. Which plane figure is a face in the three-dimensional figure?

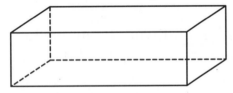

   A triangle   **B** rectangle
   C pentagon   **D** hexagon

6. Which plane figure is a face in the three-dimensional figure?

   F triangle   **G** square
   H pentagon   **J** hexagon

7. Lydia, Art, Cal, Pat, and Donna set up their tents in a circle. Lydia is between Donna and Pat. Pat is next to Cal. Who is Art between?

   A Lydia and Pat **B** Cal and Lydia
   C Donna and Pat **D** Cal and Donna

8. In the past year, Cynthia earned $290 baby-sitting, $322 mowing lawns, and $489 setting up computers. Which is the most reasonable estimate of her total earnings?

   F $600   **G** $800
   H $1,000   **J** $1,100

9. **Write About It** Describe the strategy you used to solve Problem 7.

_____

_____

More About Solid Figures

Write the correct answer.

1. I am a three-dimensional figure with 6 faces. All of my faces are congruent squares. What am I?

_____

2. I am a three-dimensional figure with 5 vertices and 5 edges. I have 1 face that is a square. What am I?

_____

3. What unit of measure would you use to measure the area of a rug? Write *ft*, *sq ft*, or *cu ft*.

_____

4. How many dimensions does a soccer ball have? Write *one-dimensional, two-dimensional,* or *three-dimensional.*

_____

Choose the correct answer

5. Which solid figure has the greatest number of faces?

   A cube
   B triangular pyramid
   C square pyramid
   D triangular prism

6. Which solid figure has only triangular faces?

   F cube
   G triangular pyramid
   H square pyramid
   J triangular prism

7. Tina wants to build a greenhouse in the shape of a square pyramid. Each triangular shape will have 42 glass tiles. How many tiles does she need?

   A 42 tiles
   B 84 tiles
   C 126 tiles
   D 168 tiles

8. What figure could be made with this net?

   F cube
   G square pyramid
   H triangular prism
   J Not Here

9. **Write About It** Describe how you solved Problem 2.

_____

_____

Plane Figures on a Coordinate Grid

Write the correct answer.

1. Mark the ordered pairs (4,1), (6,1), (8,3), (6,5), (4,5), and (2,3) on the coordinate grid. Connect the points. Write the name of the figure.

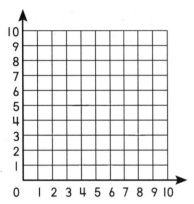

_____

2. Write the names of the faces and the number of each face on a triangular pyramid.

_____

3. Write the names of the faces and the number of each face on a pentagonal prism.

_____

Choose the letter of the correct answer.

4. How many vertices does the figure have?

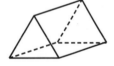

  A 6   **B** 7   **C** 8   **D** 9

5. How many edges does the figure have?

  F 6   **G** 7   **H** 8   **J** 9

6. Tasha makes a three-dimensional figure that has 6 faces. What can the figure be?

  A circle   **B** cone
  C cylinder   **D** cube

7. Roger has 3 quarters, 2 dimes, and 5 pennies. How much money does he have in all?

  F $0.95   **G** $1.00
  H $1.25   **J** Not Here

8. **Write About It** What can you conclude about a point that has 0 as one of its coordinates?

_____

Classifying and Sorting Solid Figures

Write the correct answer.

1. Write a label for each part of the Venn diagram.

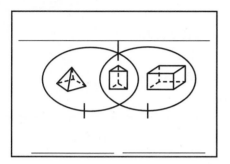

2. What solid figure can you see in the drawing?

_____

3. Name a solid figure that has 8 vertices.

_____

4. Write the names of the faces and the number of each kind of face on a triangular pyramid.

_____

Choose the letter of the correct answer.

5. Which figure has the fewest faces?

  A cube
  B triangular pyramid
  C rectangular prism
  D square pyramid

6. Wayne wants to rent a garage for storing boxes. Which unit should he use to measure its volume?

  F ft   **G** in
  H cu ft   **J** sq ft

7. Neal challenges Lynn to name a solid figure that has no edges. Lynn names one. Which figure does she name?

  A cube   **B** cone
  C cylinder   **D** sphere

8. A football team wins a national championship and 43,180 people are expected to attend the celebration. The arena holds only 22,520 people. About how many people will have to be turned away?

  F About 32,000   **G** About 18,000
  H About 20,000   **J** About 11,000

9. **Write About It** Explain how you solved Problem 8.

_____

_____

Name _____

Making Generalizations

Generalizations are from experiences or pieces of
information used to draw conclusions. Generalizations
may use words such as many or most. Read the following
problem.

> Neil is going on a camping trip. He will take with him
> tuna, cereal, paper towels, a flashlight, a baseball,
> matches, and a teepee-styled tent. Sort the objects by
> the three-dimensional figures they suggest.

1. Use what you know about each object to make a generalization. Complete
the chart.

OBJECT	GENERALIZATION
tuna	Most tuna comes in cans.

2. Solve the problem. _____

_____

_____

3. Describe the strategy you used. _____

_____

Use what you know about each object to make a generalization. Solve.

4. Andrea takes an ice chest, a beach   _____
ball, a book, some cans of soda, a
sandwich, a bottle of water, a raft,   _____
and a sand bucket with her to the
beach. Sort the objects by the   _____
three-dimensional figures they
suggest.   _____

                                           _____

Name _____

Line Segments

Write the correct answer.

1. Write *parallel* or *not parallel* to describe the line segments.

_____

2. Write *line segment* or *not a line segment* to describe the figure.

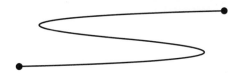

_____

3. Write the name of the solid figure that has one square face and four triangular faces.

_____

4. Write the name of the solid figure that has one curved surface and two circular faces.

_____

Choose the letter of the correct answer.

5. Which name describes the figure?

A point   **B** line
C line segment **D** plane

6. Which name describes the figure?

F point   **G** line
H line segment **J** plane

7. Two yellow lines are painted along the center of a straight stretch of highway. Which description is most reasonable for the lines?

A planes
B not parallel
C points
D parallel

8. Allan counts the pendulum swings on his grandfather clock. He counts 60 swings in 1 minute. How many times does the pendulum swing in 1 second?

F 2 time   **G** 30 times
H 1 time   **J** Not Here

9. **Write About It** Describe the method you used to solve Problem 8.

_____

_____

_____

Name _____

Exploring Angles and Line Relationships

Write the correct answer.

1. Write the name that best describes the line relationship: *parallel* or *intersecting*.

_____

2. Which figure does the surface of this sheet of paper most resemble: a point, a line, a line segment, or a plane?

_____

3. Write *acute, obtuse,* or *right* to describe the angles formed by the lines in Problem 1.

_____

4. Which figure does the answer blank below most resemble: a point, a line, a line segment, or a plane?

_____

Choose the letter of the correct answer.

5. Which name describes the angle?

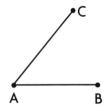

A acute   B obtuse
C right   D parallel

6. Which name describes the lines?

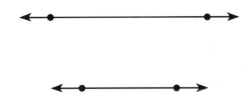

F acute   G parallel
H intersecting   J Not Here

7. Tabitha draws two perpendicular lines. Which statement about the lines is *not* true?

A They form four angles.
B They form four right angles.
C They intersect.
D They are parallel.

8. Ned has five coins in his pocket. Which amount cannot be the total value of the coins?

F $1.05   G $0.25
H $0.29   J $0.20

9. **Write About It** Describe the strategy you used to solve Problem 7.

_____

_____

More About Angles and Line Relationships

Write the correct answer.

1. Write the name that best describes the line relationship: *parallel*, *perpendicular*, or *intersecting*.

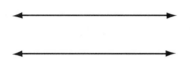

_____

2. Write the name that best describes the line relationship: *parallel*, *perpendicular*, or *intersecting*.

_____

3. Write *acute, obtuse,* or *right* to describe the angles formed by the lines in Problem 2.

_____

4. Write *points, lines,* or *line segments,* to describe the figures in Problem 1.

_____

Choose the letter of the correct answer.

5. Which name describes the angle?

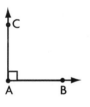

   A acute   B obtuse
   C right   D parallel

6. Which name describes the figure?

   X━━━━━━━━Y

   F plane   G line segment
   H point   J line

7. Emilio draws two parallel lines. Which statement about the lines is true?

   A They form two angles.
   B They form four acute angles.
   C They intersect.
   D They do not intersect.

8. Which figure cannot be one of the faces of a rectangular prism?

   F rectangle
   G square
   H circle
   J Not Here

9. **Write About It** Describe the strategy you used to solve Problem 8.

_____

_____

Polygons

Write the correct answer.

1. Write *polygon* or *not a polygon* to describe the figure.

   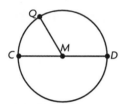

   _____

2. Name the polygon and tell how many sides and angles it has.

   _____

3. Name the diameter of the circle.

   _____

4. Name each radius in the circle in Problem 3.

   _____

Choose the letter of the correct answer.

5. Which is the correct name for the polygon?

   A quadrilateral
   B pentagon
   C hexagon
   D octagon

6. Keith draws a polygon that has 8 angles. Which is the correct name for the polygon?

   F quadrilateral   G pentagon
   H hexagon   J octagon

7. Floyd sets out on an 11-mile hike at 9:15 A.M. He walks at a rate of 15 minutes per mile. If he stops halfway for 45 minutes to have lunch, what time does he finish his hike?

   F Noon   G 12:45 p.m.
   H 1:15 p.m.   J Not Here

8. The Mervin family took a 6-day vacation. Each day, they drove twice as far as they had driven the day before. If they drove 12 miles on the first day, how far did they drive during their entire vacation?

   A 384 mi   B 592 mi
   C 1,244 mi   D 756 mi

9. **Write About It** Explain how you solved Problem 7.

   _____

   _____

   _____

Name _____

Quadrilaterals

Write the correct answer.

1. This quadrilateral has 2 pairs of parallel sides. Its opposite sides are congruent. It has no right angles. What quadrilateral is it?

_____

2. Name the quadrilateral shown below.

_____

3. Harold notices that a "Road Slippery When Wet" sign has 5 angles. What kind of polygon is it?

_____

4. Pies are usually sliced from the center out to the edge. What part of a circle does such a cut make?

_____

Choose the letter of the correct answer.

5. Which of these lines and angles are *not* in the figure below?

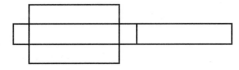

   A parallel lines
   B right angles
   C perpendicular lines
   D acute angles

6. Which solid figure could you create by cutting out and folding the pattern in Problem 5?

   F square pyramid
   G cube
   H rectangular prism
   J triangular prism

7. Bart walks some of his neighbors' dogs to make extra money. He takes 12 dogs for walks. Each dog gets 2 walks a day. How many walks does he take in a week?

   A 148 walks   B 180 walks
   C 124 walks   D 168 walks

8. **Write About It** Explain why this statement is true. All squares are rectangles but not all rectangles are squares.

_____

_____

_____

_____

Synthesizing Ideas/Information

To **synthesize** means to form a whole by combining parts. You can combine, or put together, ideas, information, or objects to make something different from the separate parts. Read the following problem.

VOCABULARY

synthesize

> There are 5 animal cages in a row at the Pretty Pet Parlor. The poodle is on the far left. The boxer is in the middle. The Labrador is next to the boxer. The greyhound is between the poodle and the boxer. Where is the Chihuahua?

1. Synthesize the parts to form the whole. Identify each part and the information given about that part. Complete the table.

PART (DOG)	INFORMATION
Poodle	on the far left
Boxer	
Labrador	
Greyhound	

2. Solve the problem. _____

3. Describe the strategy you used. _____

_____

Synthesize the parts of each problem. Solve.

4. Annsil has 2 one-dollar bills, 1 half dollar, 7 quarters, 6 dimes, and 3 nickels. She wants to have just one bill and no change. Can she do this with the money she has? Explain.

_____

_____

5. Trace and cut out the 6 puzzle parts. Make a triangle using only the 4 smaller parts. Then make a square using all the parts. Draw pictures of the triangle and square.

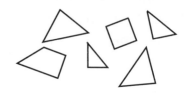

PS68   READING STRATEGY

Finding Perimeter

Write the correct answer.

1. Write the perimeter.

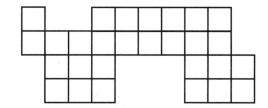

_____

2. Write the perimeter.

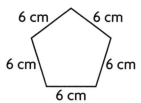

6 cm   6 cm

6 cm   6 cm

6 cm

_____

3. Name the quadrilateral that has two pairs of parallel sides. All sides may or may not be of equal length. All angles may or may not be right angles.

_____

4. Write the names of the faces and the number of each face on a triangular prism.

_____

Choose the letter of the correct answer.

5. Which of these solid figures has the greatest number of vertices?

A square pyramid

B cube

C triangular pyramid

D triangular prism

7. Gina puts on a CD at 7:35 P.M. She plays one half of the CD, then pauses the player at 8:10 P.M. How many minutes of music are there on the CD?

A 35 min   B 60 min

C 75 min   D 70 min

6. Which name best describes the lines formed by the two rails on a straight stretch of railroad track?

F perpendicular   G parallel

H intersecting   J obtuse

8. Steven's living room has an L-shaped layout. He measures four of the walls. They measure 12 ft, 14 ft, 14 ft, and 12 ft. The perimeter of the room is 104 ft. If the last two walls have the same length, what is the length of each?

F 52 ft   G 22 ft

H 26 ft   J Not Here

9. Write About It Describe the method you used to solve Problem 8.

_____

_____

Area of Irregular Figures

Write the correct answer.

1. Estimate the area of the figure in square units.

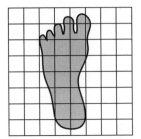

_____

2. Estimate the area of the figure in square units.

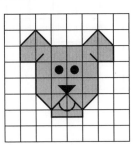

_____

3. A house in the shape of a rectangle measures 50 feet by 24 feet. What is the the perimeter of the house?

_____

4. Name the quadrilateral that has exactly 2 parallel sides.

_____

Choose the letter of the correct answer.

5. Which of these categories do squares *not* belong to?

   A rectangles   B parallelograms
   C trapezoids   D quadrilaterals

7. Evan wants to estimate the area of a shape. He traces it on grid paper. There are 58 squares that are partially covered by the shape. There are 42 squares that are fully covered by the shape. Which is the most reasonable estimate of the shape's area?

   A 100 sq units   B 2,400 sq units
   C 79 sq units   D 71 sq units

6. Which of these figures has 5 faces, with 4 of the faces being triangles?

   F square pyramid
   G cube
   H triangular prism
   J triangular pyramid

8. Maya bought 32 megabytes of RAM memory for her computer for a total of $192. Kayla bought 16 megabytes of RAM memory for a total of $80. How much less per megabyte did Kayla pay?

   F $4.00 less   G $0.50 less
   H $2.00 less   J $1.00 less

9. **Write About It** Describe the method you used to estimate the area in Problem 7.

_____

_____

Name _____

Finding Area

Write the correct answer.

1. Write the area of the rectangle.

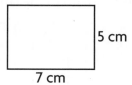

5 cm

7 cm

_____

2. Write the area of the rectangle.

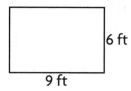

6 ft

9 ft

_____

3. What is the perimeter of a garden that has sides that measure 36 ft, 18 ft, 28 ft, 19 ft, and 17 ft?

_____

4. Name the solid figure that has one flat face and one curved surface.

_____

Choose the letter of the correct answer.

5. Which solid figure has fewer than eight edges?

   A triangular prism
   B cube
   C square pyramid
   D triangular pyramid

6. Which term best describes the figure shown in Problem 2?

   F one-dimensional
   G two-dimensional
   H three-dimensional
   J four-dimensional

7. Rhonda traces the area covered by a lake, from a map onto grid paper. Which is the most reasonable estimate of the area of the lake on the map?

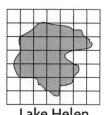

Lake Helen

   A 8 sq units
   B 12 sq units
   C 19 sq units
   D 26 sq units

8. How many four-digit numbers can you make using the digits 1, 2, 3, and 4 without repeating any of the digits in the same number?

   F 12 numbers
   G 10 numbers
   H 24 numbers
   J Not Here

9. **Write About It** Explain how you chose the most reasonable estimate in Problem 7.

_____

_____

Relating Area and Perimeter

Write the correct answer.

1. Write the perimeter and the area
   of the figure.

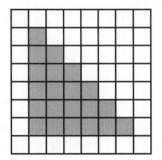

_____

2. Which two figures have the same
   area but different perimeters?

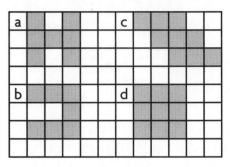

_____

3. Nadia's parents are carpeting their
   family room. The room is a
   rectangle that measures 6 yard
   by 5 yard. How many square yards
   of carpeting do they need?

_____

4. Pete walks to the intersection of
   two roads. He notices that the
   corner he is standing on is a right
   angle. What type of intersecting
   lines do the roads form?

_____

Choose the letter of the correct answer.

5. Which of these letters is not
   formed entirely of line segments?

   A A   B X   C Y   D R

6. Which solid figure does not have a
   curved surface?

   F cylinder   G cube
   H sphere   J cone

7. At 9:00 P.M. the temperature is
   55°F. By midnight it has dropped
   to 34°F. If it continues falling at
   the same rate, what will the
   temperature be at 4:00 A.M.?

   A 7°F   B 13°F
   C 9°F   D 6°F

8. Les is cutting polygons out of
   paper. He cuts the four corners
   off of a square. What polygon is
   left?

   F rectangle   G octagon
   H hexagon   J Not Here

9. **Write About It** What strategy did you use to solve
   Problem 8? Explain.

_____

_____

Observing Relationships

It is helpful to **observe relationships** when trying to solve some problems. When finding the greatest possible area of rectangles that have the same perimeter, observe the relationship between the area of each rectangle as the width and length change. Read the following problem.

VOCABULARY
observe relationships

> Pandora has 48 feet of fencing to build a play space for her dog. She wants to give her dog the greatest possible area. What is the greatest possible area that Pandora can make?

---

1. Observe the relationship between the side measurements and the area of different rectangles having a perimeter of 48 feet. Draw and complete the table.

Width (ft)	Length (ft)	Difference	Area
1	23	$23 - 1 = 22$	23 sq ft
2	22		
3			

2. As the difference between the width and the length becomes less, what happens to the area? _____

3. How can this relationship between the measurements of the sides and the area help you find the greatest area? _____

_____

4. Solve the problem. _____

5. Describe another strategy you could have used. _____

_____

Observe relationships in each problem. Solve.

6. Hector has 56 feet of wire to put around a flower garden. He wants to plant flowers in the greatest possible area. What is the greatest possible area that Hector can make his garden?

7. Sandy has 96 feet of fencing to build a corral for her pony. She wants to give her pony the greatest possible area she can. What is the greatest possible area that Sandy can make the corral?

_____   _____

Translations, Reflections, and Rotations

Write the correct answer.

1. Write *translation, reflection,* or *rotation* to describe how the shaded figure was moved to the position of the unshaded figure.

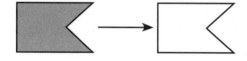

_____

2. Write *translation, reflection,* or *rotation* to describe how the unshaded figure was moved to form the shaded figure.

_____

3. A rectangular patio measures 8 feet × 9 feet. How many square feet of outdoor carpeting are needed to cover the patio?

_____

4. Lyle is putting up fencing around a five-sided wooded area. The sides measure 22 yards, 18 yards, 30 yards, 19 yards, and 11 yards. How much fencing will Lyle need for the area?

_____

Choose the letter of the correct answer.

5. What is the perimeter of a hexagon that measures 8 cm on each side?

A 64 cm   B 48 cm
C 32 cm   D 16 cm

6. What is the area of a rectangle that measures 10 meters by 5 meters?

F 100 sq m   G 40 sq m
H 30 sq m   J 50 sq m

7. Betty has 6 horses. She wants each horse to have at least 15,000 square yards of space to graze. Which enclosures will have enough room for all 6 horses? Use a calculator.

A 150 yd × 300 yd
B 200 yd × 250 yd
C 250 yd × 300 yd
D 300 yd × 300 yd

8. **Write About It** Describe the steps you took to solve Problem 7.

_____

_____

_____

_____

_____

Name _____

Congruence

Write the correct answer.

1. Write *congruent* or *not congruent* to describe the two figures.

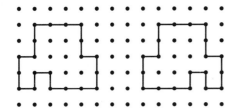

_____

2. Write *congruent* or *not congruent* to describe the two figures.

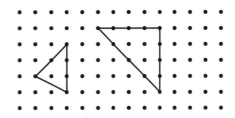

_____

3. Write *translation, reflection,* or *rotation* to describe how the figure on the left was moved to form the figure on the right in Problem 1 above.

_____

4. How many square yards of tile are needed to cover the floor of a rectangular kitchen that measures 3 yard along one edge and 5 yard along another?

_____

Choose the letter of the correct answer.

5. Which kinds of lines always form four right angles?

   A parallel   **B** intersecting
   C congruent   **D** perpendicular

6. Which kind of angle does the corner of a rectangle form?

   F right   **G** acute
   H obtuse   **J** parallel

7. The word *kilobyte* means "one thousand bytes" of information. But a kilobyte is actually 1,024 bytes of information. How many more actual bytes are there in a kilobyte of information?

   A 2 bytes   **B** 16 bytes
   C 24 bytes   **D** 1,000 bytes

8. Which of the following does *not* have to be true about two congruent figures?

   F They have the same area.
   G They have equal perimeters.
   H They have the same number of sides.
   J Not Here

9. **Write about It** Explain why you chose the answer you did in Problem 7.

_____

_____

Two Kinds of Symmetry

Write the correct answer.

1. Does the figure have point
   symmetry? Write yes or no.

   _____

2. Does the figure have point
   symmetry? Write yes or no.

   _____

3. Maura's bedroom is a 10-foot by
   13-foot rectangle. Her brother's
   bedroom is a 13-foot by 10-foot
   rectangle. Are the floors of the
   two rooms congruent?

   _____

4. I am a polygon with 5 sides and
   5 angles. What polygon am I?

   _____

Choose the letter of the correct answer.

5. Which quadrilateral has four
   congruent sides and four right
   angles?

   A rectangle   B trapezoid
   C parallelogram   D square

6. What is the number of angles in
   an octagon?

   F 4   G 5
   H 6   J 8

7. Larry is using four triangles and a
   square as the faces for a birdhouse
   he is making. Which shape could
   the birdhouse have when Larry
   assembles it?

   A triangular prism
   B triangular pyramid
   C pentagonal prism
   D square pyramid

8. Lines AB and CD are parallel.
   Which of the following do you also
   know is true about them?

   F They are intersecting.
   G They are perpendicular.
   H They do not meet.
   J Not Here

9. **Write About It** Describe the method you used to test for
   point symmetry in Problems 1 and 2.

   _____

   _____

Tesselations

Write the correct answer.

1. Write *will tessellate* or *will not* tessellate to describe the figure.

_____

2. Write the names of the polygons that tessellate in the design.

_____

3. Write *yes* or *no* to tell whether the dashed line is a line of symmetry.

_____

4. Write *yes* or *no* to tell whether the figure has point symmetry.

_____

Choose the letter of the correct answer.

5. Woody wants to wallpaper a wall that is 8 ft high by 9 ft wide. How much wallpaper does he need?

   A 17 sq ft   B 72 sq ft
   C 144 sq ft   D 36 sq ft

6. Which quadrilateral has four right angles and has its opposite sides parallel and congruent?

   F rhombus   G parallelogram
   H square   J trapezoid

7. A farmer wants to make a rectangular pen in one of his fields. He has 72 feet of fencing. Which size pen can he make?

   A 19 ft × 19 ft   B 20 ft × 19 ft
   C 18 ft × 18 ft   D 20 ft × 18 ft

8. Jacqueline notices a pattern in the areas of some rectangles: 12 square feet, 24 square feet, and 36 square feet. Which area should come next in the pattern?

   F 48 sq ft   G 52 sq ft
   H 96 sq ft   J Not Here

9. **Write About It** Give the rule for the pattern you saw in Problem 8.

_____

Changing the Sizes of Shapes

Write the correct answer.

1. Write *similar* or *not similar* to
   describe the two figures.

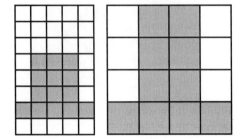

_____

2. Write *congruent* or *not congruent*
   to describe the two figures.

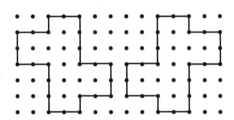

_____

3. Look again at the two figures in
   Problem 2. Write *translation*,
   reflection, or *rotation* to describe
   how the left figure was moved to
   form the right figure.

_____

4. Look again at the two figures in
   Problem 2. Are the figures similar?

_____

Choose the letter of the correct answer.

5. Wally rents a rectangular studio
   apartment that measures 5 yard by
   7 yard. How much carpeting will
   he need to cover the floor?

   A 12 sq yd   B 24 sq yd
   C 35 sq yd   D 70 sq yd

6. The Thomsons build a new house
   that has 8 sides. What is the name
   of the polygon that describes the
   shape of their house?

   F trapezoid   G pentagon
   H octagon   J hexagon

7. Laverne is retiling her bathroom.
   Which shape of tile could not be
   used to cover the entire floor?

   A hexagons   B squares
   C rectangles   D pentagons

8. A dealer sells a car for $14,998.
   She makes a $825 profit on the
   car. How much did the dealer pay
   for the car?

   F $15,823   G $14,273
   H $14,173   J $15,723

9. **Write About It** Explain why Laverne cannot use the tile
   shape you chose in Problem 7.

_____

_____

Paraphrasing

Sometimes it is helpful to **paraphrase**, or state again in your own words, what a problem is asking you to do. Read the following problem.

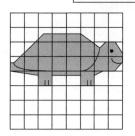

Suppose you want to make a larger copy of the picture of the turtle at the right. How could you make a copy of the figure, square by square, and make a larger picture?

1. Complete the sentence to paraphrase what the problem is asking you to do.

The problem asks me to _____

_____

2. Solve the problem. _____

_____

3. Describe the strategy you used. _____

_____

Paraphrase what each problem is asking you to do. Solve.

4. Suppose you want to make a larger picture of the cat at the right. Use one-inch grid paper. Then copy the figure, square by square, to make a larger picture.

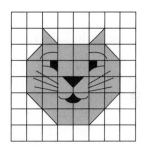

5. Suppose you want to make a larger picture of the emblem at the right. Use one-inch grid paper. Then copy the figure, square by square, to make a larger picture.

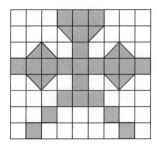

Name _____

Multiplying by Multiples

Write the correct answer.

1. Write the missing number to finish the pattern.

$$3 \times 50 = 150$$
$$3 \times 500 = 1,500$$
$$3 \times 5,000 = \underline{\ ?\ }$$

_____

2. Write the missing number to finish the pattern.

$$5 \times 90 = 450$$
$$5 \times 900 = 4,500$$
$$5 \times \underline{\ ?\ } = 45,000$$

_____

3. Use mental math and patterns of zeros to find the product.

$$8 \times 700 = \underline{\ ?\ }$$

_____

4. What is the perimeter of a square with sides that are 6 feet in length?

_____

Choose the letter of the correct answer.

5. Which number completes the multiplication sentence?

$$8 \times \underline{\ ?\ } = 7,200$$

A 9,000   **B** 900   **C** 600   **D** 60

6. Which number completes the multiplication sentence?

$$\underline{\ ?\ } \times 700 = 6,300$$

F 6   **G** 9   **H** 8   **J** 7

7. Ralph goes to the movies with a friend. He buys 2 tickets for $7.50 each. He also buys a $3.50 bucket of popcorn and a $2.25 cup of soda. He has $3.50 left when he gets home. How much did he have when he went to the movies?

A $24.25   **B** $16.75
C $25.75   **D** $19.50

8. Lila puts the coins from her coin jar into rolls. She has 9 rolls of quarters. Each roll holds 40 quarters. She has 7 rolls of nickels. Each roll holds 40 nickels. What is the total value of her rolls of coins?

F $44   **G** $36
H $104   **J** Not Here

9. **Write About It** Describe the strategy you used to solve Problem 8.

_____

_____

_____

PS80   PROBLEM SOLVING

Modeling Multiplication

Write the correct answer.

1. Solve.

$$\begin{array}{r} 76 \\ \times\ 4 \\ \hline \end{array}$$

_____

2. Solve.

$$7 \times 37 = \underline{\ ?\ }$$

_____

3. The Lancaster School has 5 fourth-grade classes. Each of the classes has 20 students. Write the total number of fourth-grade students at the Lancaster School.

_____

4. Seven volunteers are collecting voter signatures on a petition. Each volunteer collected 600 signatures. Write the total number of signatures collected.

_____

Choose the letter of the correct answer.

5. $9 \times 54 = \underline{\ ?\ }$

A 438   **B** 486   **C** 516   **D** 36

6. $4 \times 87 = \underline{\ ?\ }$

F 348   **G** 378   **H** 398   **J** 328

7. Papa Joe's Café serves sandwiches with fried chicken, chicken steak, barbecued flank, or catfish. They serve their sandwiches on white bread, rye bread, or a roll. How many different sandwich choices are there?

A 7   **B** 12
C 8   **D** 24

8. Dr. Stephanie sees 36 patients each day. She has to write out 4 different forms for each patient. How many forms does she have to write out for the day?

F 68   **G** 256
H 144   **J** 112

9. Write About It Describe the strategy you used to solve Problem 7.

_____

_____

Recording Multiplication

Write the correct answer.

1. Write the place-value positions you need to regroup to multiply 5×154.

   _____

2. Solve.

   $$\begin{array}{r} 238 \\ \times 3 \\ \hline \end{array}$$

   _____

3. The New Bedford Soccer League has 6 teams. Each team has 13 players. How many players are there in the New Bedford Soccer League?

   _____

4. The Century Scholarship Fund gives out 8 scholarships each year. If each of the scholarships is worth $5,000, how much money does the fund give out each year?

   _____

Choose the letter of the correct answer.

5. $4 \times 129 = \underline{\ ?\ }$

   A 516   **B** 486   **C** 496   **D** 506

6. $$\begin{array}{r} 317 \\ \times 3 \\ \hline \end{array}$$

   F 931   **G** 981   **H** 921   **J** 951

7. Eileen is a marathon runner. Each weekday, she runs 13 miles. Each Saturday and Sunday, she runs 17 miles. How much farther does she run in all during the 5 weekdays than she runs on Saturday and Sunday?

   A 99 mi   **B** 65 mi
   C 31 mi   **D** 55 mi

8. Every time Chris shovels Mrs. Barr's driveway after every snowfall, she deposits $9 into Chris's college tuition fund. During the winter, it snowed 27 times. How much money did Mrs. Barr deposit into Chris's college tuition fund?

   F $270   **G** $234
   H $243   **J** Not Here

9. **Write About It** Describe the steps you took to solve Problem 7.

   _____

   _____

   _____

Practicing Multiplication

Write the correct answer.

1. Solve.

$$\$2.77 \times 3$$

_____

2. Solve.

$$\begin{array}{r} \$3.98 \\ \times \quad 4 \\ \hline \end{array}$$

_____

3. Nathan decides to write a book about his experiences in fourth grade. He plans to write at least 250 words each day. After 5 days of writing, what is the least number of words he should have?

_____

4. Maura reads that there are an average of 3 radios for every person in the country. She lives in a town of about 7,000 people. About how many radios can she expect there to be in her town?

_____

Choose the letter of the correct answer.

5.
$$\begin{array}{r} \$9.05 \\ \times \quad 7 \\ \hline \end{array}$$

A $56.35   B $72.42
C $58.55   D $63.35

6. Which number completes the pattern?

$$8 \times 40 = 320$$
$$8 \times \underline{\ ?\ } = 3,200$$
$$8 \times 4,000 = 32,000$$

F 4   G 40   H 400   J 4,000

7. Ellen builds an electric motor from a kit. She winds 500 turns of wire in a coil to make an electromagnet. She estimates there is about 2 inches of wire in each turn. About how many inches of wire did she use?

A 750 in.   B 900 in.
C 1,000 in.   D 1,100 in.

8. Liang moves to a new home. He packs his tapes in 3 boxes of 8 tapes each. He also puts 6 tapes in a bag. Which number sentence can you use to find out how many tapes Liang owns?

F $3 \times 8 + 6$ G $6 - 3 \times 8$
H $5 \times 6 - 3$ J $5 + 6 + 3$

9. **Write About It** Describe the steps you took to solve Problem 7.

_____

_____

Interpreting Symbols

It is important to be able to interpret symbols when
reading or writing a number sentence. **Interpreting
symbols** means understanding what each symbol in the
number sentence means. Some mathematical symbols are
$+$, $-$, $\times$, $\div$, $=$, and n. Read the following problem.

VOCABULARY

interpreting
symbols

> Alex bought 4 computer games. Each game cost $39.95.
> How much money did Alex spend?

---

1. Interpret each symbol in the number sentence. Write the
   meaning beneath each symbol.

   ___4___   ___×___   ___$39.95___   ___=___   ___n___

   number   _____   cost per   _____   _____
   of games   _____   game   _____   _____

2. Solve the problem. _____

3. Describe the strategy you used. _____

   _____

Write a number sentence for each problem. Interpret what each
symbol means. Solve.

4. Stan spent $238.50 on computer
   programs. Stella spent $152.75 on
   computer programs. How much
   more did Stan spend than Stella?

5. Jody spends 125 minutes a day, 3
   days a month, on the Internet.
   How much time each month does
   Jody spend on the Internet?

   _____

   _____   _____

   _____   _____

   _____   _____

   _____   _____

Patterns with Multiples

Write the correct answer.

1. Write the missing number to finish the pattern.

$$4 \times 70 = 280$$
$$40 \times 70 = 2,800$$
$$40 \times 700 = \underline{\ ?\ }$$

_____

2. Solve.

$$\begin{array}{r} 800 \\ \times\ 60 \\ \hline \end{array}$$

_____

3. Hal brings 8 rolls of dimes to the bank. Each roll holds 50 dimes. How many $20 bills should the bank give Hal for his rolls of dimes?

_____

4. Carla's favorite piece of music is about 17 minutes long. She has the music on a CD. She likes to play it over and over again. About how long does it take her to listen to it 9 times?

_____

Choose the letter of the correct answer.

5. Which number will complete the pattern?

$$6 \times 90 = 540$$
$$60 \times 90 = 5,400$$
$$60 \times \underline{\ ?\ } = 54,000$$

A 9 **B** 90 **C** 900 **D** 9,000

6. Which of these words has two lines of symmetry?

F MOM **G** DAD
H BODE **J** OHO

7. Which product completes the number sentence?

$$50 \times 7,000 = \underline{\ ?\ }$$

A 3,500 **B** 35,000
C 42,000 **D** 350,000

8. Six partners agree to start a business together. Each partner will contribute $4,000 toward the business. The business will also take out a $15,000 loan. How much money will the business have?

F $19,000 **G** $24,000
H $39,000 **J** Not Here

9. **Write About It** Describe the pattern of zeros that you could use to solve Problem 7.

_____

_____

_____

Name _____

Using a Glossary

A **glossary** is a set of special terms and their definitions, often found at the back of a book. Read the following problem.

> Isaac is reading a science fiction book with several unfamiliar terms. He reads that 800 Venusian vultags live in the dark Caravian Cave. Their many eyes reflect the light from Zoran's torch. How many eyes are reflecting light?

1. Use the glossary below. Underline the term and definition you need to solve the problem.

Glossary
android: an automaton, or robot, in the form of a human being.
Andromeda: a northern constellation between Pisces and Cassiopeia.
dromed: a special android with 40 extensions. Dromeds are often used to repair space ships. They come from Andromeda.
Kryos crystal: a crystal generating great power when activated. The correct numbers to activate the crystal are 24, 33, and 8.
vultag: a birdlike creature inhabiting Venus. It is similar to the vulture found on Earth, except that it is much larger and has 30 eyes.

2. Solve the problem. _____

3. Describe the strategy you used. _____

_____

Use the glossary to define unfamiliar terms. Solve.

4. Isaac reads that Zoran is told to push 32, 41, and 16 to activate the Kryos crystal. Zoran knows the message is in code. He follows a special pattern and pushes the correct numbers to activate the Kryos crystal. What pattern did Zoran follow?

5. Isaac reads that 70 Andromeda dromeds are repairing the space ship. Because of their many extensions, the repairs are almost completed. Isaac wonders how many extensions are working on the ship. How many extensions are there in all?

Name _____

Estimating Products with Multiples

Write the correct answer.

1. Round each factor to the nearest ten, and then estimate the product.

$$56 \\ \times\ 34$$

_____

2. Round each factor, and then estimate the product.

$$481 \\ \times\ \ 18$$

_____

3. The Rocky Glen Amusement Park is open for 70 days during the summer. About 800 children visit the park every day. About how many children visit the park during the summer?

_____

4. A half gallon of milk weighs about 64 oz. Geraldo picks up a crate that holds 8 half gallons of milk. Write about how much the crate weighs in ounces.

_____

Choose the letter of the correct answer.

5. Which is the most reasonable estimate of the product?

$$166 \\ \times\ \ 84$$

A 9,000   **B** 16,000
C 7,200   **D** 1,600

6. Which is the most reasonable estimate of the product?

$$28 \times 910$$

F 27,000   **G** 2,700
H 18,000   **J** 1,800

7. Jennifer has a set of tiles that are all the same size. She arranges them in a rectangular design that has a perimeter of 38 tiles. Which choice could be the number of tiles she has?

A 24   **B** 48
C 36   **D** 52

8. There are 276 students in Norris Elementary. The cafeteria manager estimates that each student uses about 28 napkins a month at lunch. Which crate of napkins should she order for next month's supply?

F The 500-napkin crate
G The 1,000-napkin crate
H The 10,000-napkin crate
J The 20,000-napkin crate

9. Write About It Explain how you chose your answer to Problem 7.

_____

_____

_____

Recording Multiplication

Write the correct answer.

1. Solve.

$$\begin{array}{r} 74 \\ \times\ 23 \\ \hline \end{array}$$

_____

2. Solve.

$$36 \times 48 = \underline{\ ?\ }$$

_____

3. Each bag holds about 18 oranges. A store gets a shipment of 42 bags of oranges. About how many oranges are in the shipment?

_____

4. If a school bus can carry 40 students, how many students can 40 buses carry?

_____

Choose the letter of the correct answer.

5. $87 \times 44 = \underline{\ ?\ }$

   A 348,348   **B** 4,268
   C 2,848   **D** 3,828

6. What is the most reasonable estimate of 78×78?

   F About 6,400   **G** About 49,000
   H About 64,000 **J** About 640

7. A *pica* is a unit of measure used by book designers. A page in a book of poems has 1 line of text per pica. There are 26 lines of text on the page. The top and bottom margins of the page are each 6 picas. How many picas high is the page?

   A 46   **B** 54
   C 26   **D** 38

8. There are 36 inches in 1 yard. How many square inches are there in 1 square yard?

   F 36 sq in.
   G 108 sq in.
   H 1,296 sq in.
   J Not Here

9. Write About It Describe how you found the number of square inches in a square yard in Problem 8.

_____

_____

Practicing Multiplication

Write the correct answer.

1. Solve.

$$711$$
$$\times\ \ 55$$

_____

2. Solve.

$$39 \times \$23.71 = \underline{\ ?\ }$$

_____

3. Suppose your heart beats about 67 times per minute. Estimate the number of times it beats in 1 hour.

_____

4. Judy changes her car's oil every 5,000 miles. She has changed the oil a total of 18 times since she bought the car. How many miles has she put on the car?

_____

Choose the letter of the correct answer.

5. $77 \times \$8.30 = \underline{\ ?\ }$

  A $639.10   B $5,815.81

  C $655.10   D $678.10

6. $64 \times 2,371 = \underline{\ ?\ }$

  F 132,364   G 151,744

  H 145,224   J 166,394

7. Doug's Pet Shop sells ultrasonic flea collars for $44.95. Over the past year, it has sold 93 of the collars. How much money has the shop received from the sale of the flea collars?

  A $3,970.15   B $4,180.15

  C $4,223.65   D $4,180.35

8. The moon is full about every 29 days. About how many full moons will there be in a 90-day period starting after the next full moon?

  F 4   G 2

  H 9   J Not Here

9. **Write About It** Explain how you found the answer to Problem 7.

_____

_____

Dividing with Remainders

Write the correct answer.

1. Solve.

$67 \div 9$

_____

2. Solve.

$8\overline{)54}$

_____

3. Roy is painting his house. He rents a paint sprayer for $29.95 a day. It takes him 13 days to paint the house. Write his total cost for renting the sprayer.

_____

4. Jeanna and Crystal take an 8-day bike trip. They bike 60 miles each day. Do they bike more than 500 miles?

_____

Choose the letter of the correct answer.

5. $7\overline{)43}$

   A 6   **B** 6 r4

   C 5 r7   **D** 6 r1

6. $5\overline{)38}$

   F 7 r3   **G** 6 r8

   H 7 r5   **J** 8 r2

7. A typical baby wears about 5 diapers a day for the first 2 years of life. About how many diapers does the baby need?

   A 4,000

   B 3,000

   C 7,000

   D 2,000

8. Earth's diameter is about 7,900 miles. The distance from Earth to the moon is about 30 times this diameter. Estimate the distance from Earth to the moon.

   F About 310,000 mi

   G About 31,000 mi

   H About 240,000 mi

   J Not Here

9. Write About It Describe the method you used to solve Problem 7.

_____

_____

Name _____

Division Procedures

Write the correct answer.

1. Solve.

$7\overline{)94}$

_____

2. Solve.

$3\overline{)98}$

_____

3. Mr. Butterfield bakes a batch of 48 cookies for his 5 children. If each child gets the same number of cookies, how many will be left over?

_____

4. Outer space is not very far from where you are right now. At a speed of 60 miles per hour, you could travel out of the Earth's atmosphere in about 10 hours. Estimate this distance.

_____

Choose the letter of the correct answer.

5. $6\overline{)75}$

   A 12 r2   **B** 12 r3
   C 15   **D** 12

6. $4\overline{)89}$

   F 22 r1   **G** 23
   H 22 r3   **J** 42 r1

7. Doctors recommend that adults drink about 64 ounces of water each day. A gallon is 128 ounces. About how many gallons of water should an adult drink in a month?

   A about 20 gal
   B about 30 gal
   C about 60 gal
   D about 15 gal

8. Sound waves travel through the air at about 1,000 feet each second. A mile is 5,280 feet. Suppose lightning and thunder occur at the same time. If you see lightning strike and hear the thunder 20 seconds later, about how many miles away from the lightning strike are you?

   F about 1 mi   **G** about 2 mi
   H about 3 mi   **J** about 4 mi

9. Write About It Explain how you estimated the first digit of the quotient in Problem 6.

_____

_____

Placing the First Digit in the Quotient

Write the correct answer.

1. Write the number of digits in the quotient.

$$4\overline{)96}$$

_____

2. Solve.

$$6\overline{)822}$$

_____

3. Buster is taking a 96-mile bike trip over 3 days. If he bikes the same distance on each of the days, how far will he have to bike each day?

_____

4. When the BookPort has its books on sale for $9.99 each, Penny buys 8 books. How much do the 8 books cost her?

_____

Choose the letter of the correct answer.

5. $5\overline{)676}$

  A 125 r1   B 135 r1
  C 225 r1   D 115 r1

6. $7\overline{)449}$

  F 64 r5   G 64 r3
  H 64 r1   J 64

7. Sam plans to see a 97-minute movie at the twin theater. The movie starts at 7:45 P.M. After that he wants to see the other movie the theater is showing. Which is the earliest time the other movie could start for Sam to be able to see both movies?

  A 9:15 P.M.   B 10:35 P.M.
  C 9:05 P.M.   D 9:45 P.M.

8. To find her math grade, Edna adds up all 7 of her test scores and then divides that sum by 7. What is Edna's grade?

Test	1	2	3	4	5	6	7
Score	92	82	76	88	95	71	98

  F 86   G 88
  H 87   J Not Here

9. **Write About It** Explain how you could check your answer to Problem 5.

_____

_____

Interpreting Answers and Remainders

When dividing, it is important to understand what the answers and remainders mean. Answers that are even have no remainders. A remainder is what remains, or is left over, after you have made even groups. Read the following problem.

Dan has 83 books to place on shelves. After he places the books in equal groups on shelves, there are 5 books remaining to be placed on the bottom shelf. How many groups are there? How many books are in each group?

1. Write how many groups of books you think there could be. Divide. Then explain the meaning of the results.

Number of Groups	8		
Divide.			
Explain.	8 groups ___ in each group ___ books remaining		

2. Solve the problem. _____

3. Describe the strategy you used. _____

Divide and interpret the remainder to solve.

4. Janice has some baskets and 49 balls of yarn to sell. She has placed an equal number of balls in each basket. She has placed 4 balls on a table. How many baskets are there? How many balls are in each basket?

_____

_____

5. Pete has 91 pieces of jewelry. He has arranged most of the pieces in equal groups in display cases. He has placed 3 pieces behind the counter. There are fewer than 11 display cases. How many display cases are there? How many pieces of jewelry are in each display case?

_____

Dividing Three-Digit Numbers

Write the correct answer.

1. Write the number of digits that will be in the quotient.

   $4\overline{)871}$

2. Solve.

   $3\overline{)555}$

3. Heidi spends $8.40 on a strip of 4 Priority Mail stamps. How much does each stamp cost?

4. Sheldon's dog had to spend 12 days in a veterinary hospital. The cost was $98 each day. How much was the total hospital bill?

Choose the letter of the correct answer.

5. $6\overline{)458}$

   A 76 r2
   B 78 r2
   C 78 r4
   D 74 r4

6. $5\overline{)911}$

   F 182 r1
   G 190 r1
   H 168 r1
   J 178 r1

7. While flipping through the calendar in his date book, Matt sees this pattern: 31, 28, 31, 30, 31, 30, 31, ... Which is the next number in the pattern?

   A 30
   B 31
   C 29
   D 28

8. Raul drives his car to work and back 5 days each week. His business is 7 miles from his home. On Saturdays, he drives to the mall, which is 12 miles from his home. How many miles does Raul drive each year?

   F 6,512 mi
   G 3,360 mi
   H 3,888 mi
   J 4,888 mi

9. **Write About It** Explain the pattern you found in Problem 7.

_____

_____

_____

Practicing Division

Write the correct answer.

1. Solve.

$7\overline{)698}$

_____

2. Solve.

$6\overline{)699}$

_____

3. Grayson Park has 6 campsites. On Saturday night, 96 people use the campsites. If the same number of people use each campsite, how many use each one?

_____

4. In the story *The Princess and the Pea*, a woman sleeping on a stack of 200 mattresses still feels a pea under the bottom mattress. If each mattress is 7 inches thick, through how many inches of mattress does the princess feel the pea?

_____

Choose the letter of the correct answer.

5. $7\overline{)308}$

   A 34 r2 **B** 48 **C** 41 r3 **D** 44

6. $9\overline{)280}$

   F 32 **G** 30 **H** 31 r1 **J** 33 r5

7. The 87 fourth graders at Grace School volunteered to clean up the city's 7 parks. The same number of students will work at each park. The remaining students will deliver refreshments to the groups. How many students will be in each cleanup group. How many will deliver refreshments?

   A 12 per group; 5 on refreshments
   B 14 per group; 3 on refreshments
   C 12 per group; 3 on refreshments
   D 13 per group; 5 on refreshments

8. A store clerk makes a pyramid display of cans. The bottom layer of the pyramid is a square that is 7 cans on a side. The next layer up has 6 cans on a side. How many cans will be in the entire pyramid?

   F 85 cans
   G 28 cans
   H 140 cans
   J Not Here

9. Write About It Estimate the quotient in Problem 1. How can you use this estimate to mentally calculate the exact quotient and remainder?

_____

_____

Division Patterns to Estimate

Write the correct answer.

1. Write the number to finish the pattern.

    $240 \div 6 = 40$
    $2,400 \div 6 = 400$
    $24,000 \div 6 = \underline{\ ?\ }$

2. Four friends play a game with a deck of 52 cards. The players divide all of the cards equally. Write the number of cards each player gets.

3. Use a pattern of zeros to estimate the quotient.

    $5,520 \div 6$

4. Renee has 767 quarters. Write the value of her quarters.

Choose the letter of the correct answer.

5. What is the most reasonable estimate of the quotient?

    $4,178 \div 5$

    A 600   **B** 250   **C** 800   **D** 700

6. $7\overline{)63,000}$

    F 900   **G** 9,000   **H** 7,000   **J** 800

7. Chesterton was hit with a huge snowstorm that left an average of 2 inches of snow each hour. The storm left a total of 2 feet of snow. For how long did the storm last?

    A 24 hr
    B 12 hr
    C 18 hr
    D 36 hr

8. A train leaves a station at 8:15 A.M. It travels east for 45 minutes and stops at a station in the next time zone. Which true statement can you make about the time the train got to the second station?

    F It got there at 9:15 A.M.
    G It got there at 8:15 A.M.
    H It got there before 10:15 A.M.
    J Not Here

9. **Write About It** Describe the steps you took to solve Problem 7.

_____

_____

Zeros in Division

Write the correct answer.

1. Solve.

   $8)\overline{875}$

   _____

2. Solve.

   $6)\overline{\$9.60}$

   _____

3. The fleshy hawthorn is a small tree. One of the tallest ones is only 8 feet tall. The tallest redwood is about 360 feet tall. About how many of the fleshy hawthorns would it take to equal the height of the 360-foot redwood?

   _____

4. Coach Jared orders new uniforms for all 22 of the team members. If each uniform costs $38.85, how much will the uniforms cost altogether?

   _____

Choose the letter of the correct answer.

5. $7)\overline{764}$

   A 108
   C 109 r4

   B 109 r1
   D 111 r3

6. $4)\overline{\$8.28}$

   F $2.07   G $2.03   H 2.03   J 2.07

7. Byron uses a calculator to find the quotient $474.40 ÷ 4. His calculator shows 118.6, so this is the way Byron writes the quotient. How should he have written it?

   A $118.6
   B 118.60
   C $118.60
   D Not Here

8. At Green's Grocery, tuna is selling at 3 cans for $1.95. At O'Malley's, across the street, the same tuna is selling at 5 cans for $3.20. Which store has the better buy on the tuna, and how much would you save on each can?

   F Green's; save $0.03 per can
   G Green's; save $0.12 per can
   H O'Malley's; save $0.02 per can
   J O'Malley's; save $0.01 per can

9. **Write About It** Describe the steps you took to solve Problem 8.

   _____

   _____

Practicing Division

Write the correct answer.

1. Solve.

$8\overline{)\$41.28}$

_____

2. Solve.

$9\overline{)\$37.71}$

_____

3. If an egg weighs about 45 grams, about how much will 1 dozen eggs weigh?

_____

4. The Trueblue Theater holds 345 people. If it sold out every show during a 22-show run, how many people had tickets to the show?

_____

Choose the letter of the correct answer.

5. $4\overline{)\$22.36}$

A $5.44   **B** $5.54
C $5.59   **D** $4.55

6.   997
     $\times\ 37$

F 36,209   **G** 32,449
H 38,989   **J** 36,889

7. Harriet wants to find the cost per pound of a 5-pound bag of potatoes that is labeled $7.85. She divides $7.85 by 5 and writes her answer as $157 per pound. How should she have written her answer?

A $157.00 per lb
B 157 per lb
C $1.57 per lb
D Not Here

8. Sweet corn is priced at 3 ears for $0.99. Shawna wants to buy 14 ears for a party. How much will the corn cost?

F $17.50
G $4.95
H $5.62
J $4.62

9. Write About It Explain how you solved Problem 8.

_____

_____

Name _____

Meaning of the Remainder

Write the correct answer.

1. Nora has 373 books to put in boxes. Each box will hold 8 books. How many boxes does she need?

_____

2. A bricklayer building a chimney gets a load of 500 bricks. He uses 8 bricks in each layer of the chimney. How many layers can he complete with the load of bricks?

_____

3. Solve.

$5)\overline{\$99.65}$

_____

4. Solve.

$3)\overline{918}$

_____

Choose the letter of the correct answer.

5. Kyle works in a chair assembly shop. He gets a batch of 130 chair legs. Each chair needs 4 legs. How many legs will Kyle have left over?

A 32 legs   B 2 legs
C 33 legs   D 32 r2 legs

6. What is the most reasonable estimate?

$$7,918 \div 4$$

F 200   G 1,000
H 400   J 2,000

7. Ted notices that the 8th Avenue subway stops at 4th Street, 12th Street, 20th Street, 28th Street. Which stop should Ted expect to be the next?

A 30th Street   B 32nd Street
C 35th Street   D Not Here

8. Clive forms a design out of eight 1-foot square tiles. Which of the following can *not* be the perimeter of the design?

F 12 ft   G 14 ft
H 18 ft   J 34 ft

9. Write About It Explain how you used the remainder in Problem 1.

_____

_____

_____

Using Graphic Aids

Graphic aids such as maps and diagrams give important information for solving problems. Read the following problem.

VOCABULARY
graphic aids

Josh is conducting a survey along Grove Street, beginning at 18 Grove Street, and surveying the buildings in numerical order. He has 90 minutes before meeting his friend. It takes him 8 minutes to survey each building. How many buildings can Josh survey before his meeting? Where should he tell his friend to meet him?

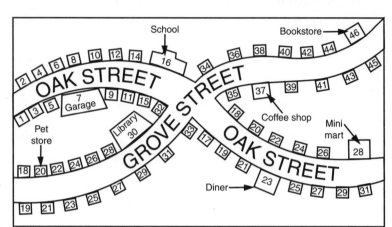

1. Use the map to help you solve the problem.

Divide to find the number of buildings Josh can survey before meeting his friend.	
He can survey _____ buildings and meet his friend on time.	
At what address will Josh be when he completes that number of surveys? _____	

2. Solve the problem. _____

_____

3. Describe the strategy you used._____

Use the map to help you solve each problem.

4. Josh conducts a survey along Oak Street. It takes him 6 minutes for each building beginning at 1 Oak Street. He has 135 minutes before meeting his father. How many buildings can Josh survey? Explain how you know and tell where his father should meet him._____

_____

Choosing the Operation

Write the correct answer.

1. Solve.

$$\begin{array}{r} 6,000 \\ \times \quad 7 \\ \hline \end{array}$$

_____

2. Solve.

$$7\overline{)35,000}$$

_____

3. The Best Friend Kennel houses about 35 pets every month. Which operation would you use to find the total number of pets they house during 1 year?

_____

4. The Smithtown Realty Company sold 192 houses last year. Which operation would you use to find the number of houses they sold each month?

_____

Choose the letter of the correct answer.

5. Which operation would you use to find the total number of customers?

AGENCY CUSTOMERS WEEK OF JAN. 15					
Day	Mon.	Tue.	Wed.	Thu.	Fri.
Customers	47	81	39	59	86

A addition   B subtraction
C multiplication   D division

6. Which operation would you use to find how many more customers the agency in Problem 5 had on Friday than on Wednesday?

F addition   G subtraction
H multiplication J division

7. Bill, Ed, Millie, and Dana sit in a row of desks. Millie sits in the front desk. Bill sits right behind Dana. Which list shows the order the four students could be seated, from front to back?

A Millie, Ed, Dana, Bill
B Millie, Dana, Ed, Bill
C Dana, Bill, Millie, Ed
D Millie, Ed, Bill, Dana

8. Quintuplets were all born within a few minutes of midnight. Chuck and Anne were born on March 31. Jill, Erin, and Ray were born on April 1. Which of the following could be the order from the youngest to the oldest?

F Erin, Jill, Anne, Ray, Chuck
G Jill, Ray, Chuck, Anne, Erin
H Jill, Erin, Ray, Chuck, Anne
J Not Here

9. **Write About It** Explain why you chose the operation you did in Problem 3.

_____

_____

Name _____

Fractions: Part of a Whole

Write the correct answer.

1. Write a fraction for the shaded part.

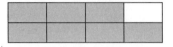

_____

2. Shade the model to show the fraction $\frac{4}{5}$.

_____

3. Write a fraction for the part of the model in Problem 1 that is *not* shaded.

_____

4. Write a fraction for the part of the figure in Problem 2 that you did *not* shade.

_____

Choose the letter of the correct answer.

5. Which fraction shows the part of the model that is shaded?

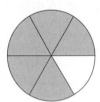

A $\frac{2}{3}$ B $\frac{3}{6}$

C $\frac{5}{6}$ D $\frac{6}{5}$

6. Which fraction shows the part of the model that is *not* shaded?

F $\frac{2}{5}$ G $\frac{5}{2}$

H $\frac{3}{5}$ J $\frac{3}{4}$

7. The Caine Building has 7 floors. A publishing company takes up 3 of the floors. An ad agency takes up 2 of the floors. A Web site design firm takes up the remaining floors in the building. What fraction of the building is used by the Web site design firm?

A $\frac{1}{7}$ B $\frac{2}{7}$

C $\frac{3}{7}$ D $\frac{4}{7}$

8. **Write About It** Explain how you chose the fraction to write for Problem 1.

_____

_____

_____

_____

_____

Name _____

Fractions: Part of a Group

Write the correct answer.

1. Write a fraction to show the part of the group that is shaded.

_____

2. Write a fraction to show the part of the whole that is shaded.

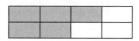

_____

3. Danny opens up a carton of eggs. He finds that 7 out of the 12 eggs are cracked. Write a fraction for the part of the group that is *not* cracked.

_____

4. Cleo cuts a pie into 6 equal slices. She eats 1 of them. Write a fraction for the part of the pie that Cleo eats.

_____

Choose the letter of the correct answer.

5. Which fraction shows the part of the group that is shaded?

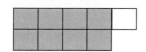

A $\frac{9}{8}$ B $\frac{1}{9}$ C $\frac{8}{17}$ D $\frac{8}{9}$

6. Which fraction shows the part of the group in Problem 5 that is *not* shaded?

F $\frac{1}{9}$ G $\frac{8}{9}$ H $\frac{1}{3}$ J $\frac{1}{10}$

7. At the Del Rey School, there are twice as many 4th graders as 5th graders. There are three times as many 6th graders as 5th graders. The total number of 4th, 5th, and 6th graders at the school is 264. How many 4th graders are there?

A 52　　　　　B 82

C 35　　　　　D 88

8. Van surveys 15 people about their opinions on a new law. Six of the people are in favor of the new law. Two of the people have no opinion. The rest are opposed to the new law. What fraction of the people she surveys are opposed?

F $\frac{6}{15}$　　　　G $\frac{2}{15}$

H $\frac{7}{15}$　　　　J Not Here

9. **Write About It** Describe the method you used to solve Problem 7.

_____

_____

Comparing and Ordering

Write the correct answer.

1. Write a number sentence using
$>$, $<$, or $=$ that compares the two
fractions shown in the models.

_____

2. Write a fraction to show the part of
the group that is shaded.

_____

3. On the soccer team, $\frac{5}{9}$ of the
players are girls. On the field
hockey team, $\frac{5}{6}$ of the players are
girls. Which team has a greater
fraction of girls?

_____

4. Leonard stood on the corner and
counted the cars that went by. Out
of 22 cars, 17 were taxis. What
fraction of the cars he saw were
taxis?

_____

Choose the letter of the correct answer.

5. Which set of fractions is ordered
from the least to the greatest?

A $\frac{2}{3}, \frac{2}{7}, \frac{2}{5}$ **B** $\frac{3}{8}, \frac{3}{7}, \frac{3}{4}$

C $\frac{1}{5}, \frac{1}{9}, \frac{1}{7}$ **D** $\frac{4}{5}, \frac{4}{7}, \frac{4}{9}$

6. Which set of fractions is ordered
from the greatest to the least?

F $\frac{3}{8}, \frac{5}{8}, \frac{7}{8}$ **G** $\frac{2}{9}, \frac{7}{9}, \frac{5}{9}$

H $\frac{1}{5}, \frac{3}{5}, \frac{4}{5}$ **J** $\frac{6}{7}, \frac{5}{7}, \frac{2}{7}$

7. In Rowayton one spring, it rained
on March 22 and every day after
that until May 2. How many days
in a row did it rain in Rowayton
that spring?

A 42 days
B 39 days
C 44 days
D 12 days

8. In Mr. Wile's class, $\frac{3}{5}$ of the
students try out for the school
play. In Ms. Kane's class, $\frac{6}{10}$ of the
students try out. In which class
does a greater fraction of the
students try out?

F Mr. Wile's   **G** Ms. Kane's
H Neither; the fractions are
    equivalent.
J Not Here

9. Write About It What rule did you use to help you order the
fractions in Problem 5?

_____

_____

Comparing and Contrasting

To solve some problems, you can compare and contrast information in a problem. Find things about the problem that are alike, and things that are different. Read the following problem.

A recipe calls for $\frac{3}{8}$ teaspoon of nutmeg, $\frac{1}{4}$ teaspoon of baking soda, and $\frac{2}{3}$ teaspoon of cinnamon. List the ingredients in order from greatest amount to least amount.

1. Write at least one way in which the fractions are alike in the **Compare** column. Write one way in which the fractions are different from each other in the **Contrast** column.

Compare	Contrast

2. Solve the problem. _____

3. Describe the strategy you used. _____

_____

Compare and contrast the fractions in each problem. Solve.

4. Lizzie has $\frac{5}{8}$ gallon of red paint, $\frac{1}{8}$ gallon of blue paint, and $\frac{3}{8}$ gallon of white paint. List the paint colors in order from least to greatest amounts.

_____

5. Scott has $\frac{3}{8}$ cup of nuts, $\frac{3}{4}$ cup of flour, and $\frac{2}{3}$ cup of sugar for baking cookies. List the ingredients in order from greatest to least amounts.

_____

6. Al made punch for a party. The recipe called for $\frac{1}{2}$ gallon of orange juice, $\frac{3}{4}$ gallon of pineapple juice, and $\frac{4}{5}$ gallon of grape juice. List the ingredients in order from greatest to least amounts.

_____

7. Karen used a recipe calling for $\frac{3}{4}$ cup of cherries, $\frac{5}{8}$ cup of water, and $\frac{1}{2}$ cup of honey. List the ingredients in order from the least to the greatest amount.

_____

Mixed Numbers

Write the correct answer.

1. Write a mixed number for the number of figures that are shaded.

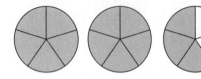

_____

2. Write a mixed number for the number of figures that are shaded.

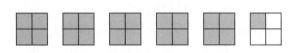

_____

3. A cake calls for 6 cups of flour. Elena uses whole wheat flour for $\frac{1}{2}$ of the recipe, white cake flour for $\frac{1}{3}$ of the recipe, and regular white flour for the remaining $\frac{1}{6}$ of the recipe. Which kind of flour does Elena use most in the cake?

_____

4. A bridge is divided into 9 equal sections. At one end of the bridge, 2 sections are over land. At the other end, 3 sections are over land. The rest are over water. What fraction of the bridge is over water?

_____

Choose the letter of the correct answer.

5. Which mixed number is equivalent to the fraction $\frac{9}{2}$?

   A 18   **B** $9\frac{1}{2}$

   C $2\frac{1}{9}$ **D** $4\frac{1}{2}$

6. Which mixed number is equivalent to the fraction $\frac{7}{3}$?

   F $7\frac{1}{3}$ **G** $3\frac{1}{7}$

   H $6\frac{1}{3}$ **J** $2\frac{1}{3}$

7. Amy plays a 30-minute cassette. The counter on her tape player moves from 0 to 360 while the tape is playing. Amy wants to play the last 10 minutes of the tape again. About how far back on the counter should she rewind the tape?

   A to 300   **B** to 240

   C to 10   **D** to 180

8. Renee bought $\frac{1}{2}$ pound of turkey, $\frac{3}{4}$ pound of cheese, and $\frac{1}{3}$ pound of tomatoes to make sandwiches. List the fractions in order from the least to the greatest.

   F $\frac{1}{3}, \frac{1}{2}, \frac{3}{4}$ **G** $\frac{3}{4}, \frac{1}{3}, \frac{1}{2}$

   H $\frac{1}{2}, \frac{3}{4}, \frac{1}{3}$ **J** Not Here

9. **Write About It** Explain how you solved Problem 7.

_____

_____

Name _____

Adding Like Fractions

Write the correct answer.

1. Use the fraction bars to help you write the sum.

$$\frac{3}{6} + \frac{2}{6}$$

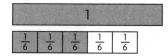

_____

2. Use the fraction bars to help you write the sum.

$$\frac{1}{8} + \frac{3}{8}$$

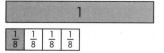

_____

3. Steven measures the thickness of a board. He records the measurement as $\frac{5}{2}$ inches. Write his measurement using a mixed number.

_____

4. Of the fourth-grade class, $\frac{5}{8}$ of the students buy milk at lunch. Of the fifth-grade class, $\frac{3}{4}$ of the students buy milk at lunch. In which grade does a greater fraction of the class buy milk?

_____

Choose the letter of the correct answer.

5. Which fraction is equivalent to $\frac{7}{8}$?

A $\frac{6}{14}$ B $\frac{8}{12}$

C $\frac{3}{4}$ D $\frac{14}{16}$

6. Which fraction is equivalent to $\frac{9}{18}$?

F $\frac{1}{2}$ G $\frac{6}{9}$

H $\frac{2}{3}$ J $\frac{27}{56}$

7. Which number comes next in the pattern?

$$\frac{1}{16}, \frac{2}{14}, \frac{3}{12}, \frac{4}{10}, \underline{\quad?\quad}$$

A $\frac{5}{9}$ B $\frac{5}{8}$

C $\frac{5}{6}$ D $\frac{5}{10}$

8. When Annette makes pumpkin pie, she adds $\frac{1}{4}$ teaspoon nutmeg, $\frac{1}{4}$ teaspoon cloves, and $\frac{1}{4}$ teaspoon allspice. What is the total amount of these three ingredients?

F $\frac{3}{8}$ teaspoon   G $\frac{3}{4}$ teaspoon

H $\frac{1}{2}$ teaspoon   J Not Here

9. **Write About It** Write a rule for the pattern you saw in Problem 7.

_____

_____

Name _____

LESSON
21.2

More About Adding Like Fractions

Write the correct answer.

1. Solve.

$$\frac{2}{7} + \frac{4}{7}$$

_____

2. Solve.

$$\frac{3}{5} + \frac{4}{5}$$

_____

3. Betty puts two strips of wood around the edge of a table. The cherry strip is $\frac{3}{4}$ inches wide, and the maple strip is $\frac{3}{8}$ inches wide. Which strip is narrower?

_____

4. Claudia's pie recipe includes $\frac{1}{8}$ teaspoon nutmeg, $\frac{1}{4}$ teaspoon cloves, and $\frac{1}{2}$ teaspoon ginger. Order the three ingredients from greatest to least.

_____

Choose the letter of the correct answer.

5. $\frac{5}{9} + \frac{8}{9} = \underline{\quad?\quad}$

  A $1\frac{3}{9}$ **B** $2\frac{1}{9}$ **C** $\frac{3}{9}$ **D** $1\frac{4}{9}$

6. $\frac{7}{10} + \frac{3}{10} = \underline{\quad?\quad}$

  F 2   **G** 1   **H** $\frac{4}{10}$ **J** $1\frac{3}{10}$

7. Tammy draws a 4-sided polygon. Its opposite sides are parallel and all sides are congruent. She measures one angle of the polygon and finds it is a right angle. Which quadrilateral has she drawn?

  A rectangle

  B square

  C triangle

  D parallelogram

8. Sheila is building bookshelves. She needs a board that is at least $1\frac{1}{2}$ in. thick. She has no boards that thick, so she decides to glue together two thinner boards. Which pair of boards can she use?

  F a $\frac{3}{8}$-in. board and a $\frac{3}{4}$-in. board

  G a $\frac{1}{8}$-in. board and a $\frac{7}{8}$-in. board

  H a $\frac{3}{4}$-in. board and a $\frac{3}{4}$-in. board

  J Not Here

9. Write About It Explain why you chose the answer you did for Problem 7.

_____

_____

_____

PS108 PROBLEM SOLVING

Name _____

Understanding Cause and Effect

A **cause** is the reason something happens. An **effect** is what happens as a result of the cause. A cause may have more than one effect. An effect may have more than one cause. Read the following problem.

VOCABULARY
cause
effect

> An ice storm caused power lines to fall down. As a result, only $\frac{1}{10}$ of the population in one town had power. The power company promised special emergency repairs if more than one half of the population lost power. What fraction of the population lost power? Will the power company make emergency repairs?

1. List the causes in the **Cause** column. List the effects in the **Effect** column.

Cause	Effect
ice storm	
Think: Did over one half of the population lose power?	Think: What will happen?

2. Solve the problem. _____

   _____

3. Describe the strategy you used. _____

   _____

List a cause and an effect in each problem. Solve.

4. Mr. Bowers tells 8 students that if more than half lost power for at least 3 days, he will postpone the math test. In the group, $\frac{2}{8}$ lost power for 1 day. The rest lost power for 3 days. Will Mr. Bowers postpone the test?

   _____

   _____

5. Ryan decided to do his homework by candlelight. Of the total time that he had, he spent $\frac{1}{5}$ doing math and $\frac{2}{5}$ doing science. The candles burned out before he had time to do English. What fraction of the time was left?

   _____

   _____

Name _____

Adding Mixed Numbers

Write the correct answer.

1. Solve.
$$2\frac{1}{8} + 3\frac{3}{8} = \underline{\ ?\ }$$

_____

2. Solve.
$$5\frac{3}{5} + 4\frac{2}{5} = \underline{\ ?\ }$$

_____

3. Neal eats $\frac{7}{8}$ of a pizza. Verne eats $\frac{6}{8}$ of a pizza. How much more pizza does Neal eat?

_____

4. Hilary finds 3 quarters in her jacket pocket. What fraction of a dollar does she have?

_____

Choose the letter of the correct answer.

5. $3\frac{1}{4} + 2\frac{2}{4} = \underline{\ ?\ }$

A $5\frac{3}{4}$

B $\frac{7}{4}$

C $\frac{8}{4}$

D 2

6. $\frac{3}{9} + \frac{2}{9} = \underline{\ ?\ }$

F $\frac{2}{9}$

G $\frac{5}{18}$

H $\frac{5}{9}$

J $1\frac{4}{5}$

7. Wendy needs a $6\frac{1}{4}$-in. piece of trim. She has a box of smaller lengths of trim. Which pair of pieces can she put together to get the length she needs?

A $3\frac{3}{4}$-in. piece and a $2\frac{3}{4}$-in. piece

B $4\frac{2}{4}$-in. piece and a $1\frac{3}{4}$-in. piece

C 2-in. piece and a $4\frac{3}{4}$-in. piece

D $3\frac{1}{4}$-in. piece and a $2\frac{3}{4}$-in. piece

8. An acre is a measure of land area. A plot of land that covers 43,560 square feet measures 1 acre. Which of the plots of land below measures closest to 1 acre?

F 160 ft × 160 ft

G 100 ft × 360 ft

H 200 ft × 220 ft

J 200 ft × 260 ft

9. **Write About It** How did you find the answer to Problem 8?

_____

_____

_____

Subtracting Mixed Numbers

Write the correct answer.

1. Solve.
$$4\frac{7}{8} - 2\frac{3}{8}$$

_____

2. Solve.
$$2\frac{1}{4} + 3\frac{3}{4}$$

_____

3. A $2\frac{1}{3}$-yard length is cut off of a $5\frac{2}{3}$-yard strip of vinyl siding. What is the length of the remaining strip of siding?

_____

4. A recipe calls for $\frac{3}{4}$ cup sugar. Emily doubles the recipe. How much sugar does she use?

_____

Choose the letter of the correct answer.

5. $8\frac{3}{5} - 7\frac{2}{5} = \underline{\ ?\ }$

A $1\frac{1}{5}$ **B** $\frac{4}{5}$ **C** $2\frac{1}{5}$ **D** $1\frac{2}{5}$

6. $5\frac{1}{10} + 5\frac{5}{10} = \underline{\ ?\ }$

F $5\frac{6}{10}$ **G** $10\frac{6}{10}$

H $\frac{60}{10}$ **J** $10\frac{4}{10}$

7. The gravity on the moon and some of the planets would make you feel lighter than you feel on Earth. Order the moon and the three planets from the one you would feel the heaviest on to the one you would feel the lightest on.

Location	Moon	Pluto	Mercury	Mars
Fraction of Weight on Earth	$\frac{17}{100}$	$\frac{4}{100}$	$\frac{37}{100}$	$\frac{38}{100}$

A Moon, Pluto, Mercury, Mars
B Pluto, Moon, Mercury, Mars
C Mars, Mercury, Pluto, Moon
D Mars, Mercury, Moon, Pluto

8. Twelve grandchildren want to chip in equal amounts to buy a gift for their grandparents' fiftieth wedding anniversary. For which gift would they be able to chip in equal whole-dollar amounts?

F an $82 silver platter
G a $90 punch bowl
H an $84 sculpture
J Not Here

9. Write About It Explain how you chose your answer to Problem 8.

_____

_____

Relating Fractions and Decimals

Write the correct answer.

1. Write the decimal for the part that is shaded.

_____

2. Write the decimal for the part that is shaded.

_____

3. In Mrs. Valerio's class, $\frac{2}{3}$ of the students bring lunch and $\frac{1}{3}$ of the students buy lunch at school. Which is greater—the fraction of the students that brings lunch or the fraction of the students that buys lunch?

_____

4. In a survey, $\frac{3}{10}$ of the people interviewed said they liked their jobs a great deal. Another $\frac{2}{10}$ said they liked their jobs somewhat. What was the total fraction of those interviewed?

_____

Choose the letter of the correct answer.

5. Which decimal is equivalent to the fraction $\frac{55}{100}$?

   A 0.5   B 5.5   C 0.55   D 0.055

6. Which fraction is equivalent to the decimal 0.24?

   F $\frac{2}{4}$ G $\frac{240}{100}$ H $\frac{24}{10}$ J $\frac{24}{100}$

7. Mike draws a square with a line connecting opposite corners. Then he draws another line connecting the other pair of opposite corners. How many triangles are there in Mike's square?

   A 4 triangles   B 6 triangles
   C 8 triangles   D 2 triangles

8. Jill and Kate have $0.60. Jill says they have 0.6 dollar. Kate says they have $\frac{3}{5}$ dollar. Who is right?

   F Jill   G Kate
   H Both   J Not Here

9. **Write About It** Explain the strategy you used to solve Problem 7.

_____

_____

_____

Tenths and Hundredths

Write the correct answer.

1. Write the decimal for the shaded part.

_____

2. Write the decimal for the shaded part.

_____

3. A library has 10 bookshelves. Each has 10 shelves in it, all the same size. Out of all of the shelves in the library, 21 hold fiction. Write a decimal to show the part of the shelves that hold fiction.

_____

4. Leo's famous chocolate chip cookie recipe calls for $2\frac{1}{2}$ cups of flour. Leo finds he has only $1\frac{1}{2}$ cups of flour. How much more flour will he need to get to make the cookies?

_____

Choose the letter of the correct answer.

5. Which decimal shows what part of a dollar 3 quarters is?

   A 0.50   B 0.25   C 0.75   D 7.5

6. Which decimal is read "three hundredths"?

   F 0.3   G 3   H 0.03   J 300

7. Gina's family moves into a new home on a 7-acre lot. The lot is in a 100-acre development. Which decimal shows what part of the 100-acre development Gina's new lot is?

   A 0.7   B 0.07
   C 0.007   D 1.7

8. James leaves his house at 8:45 A.M. to go walking. He walks steadily at about 4 miles an hour and gets back home at 10:15 A.M. About how far has he walked?

   F about 4 mi   G about 5 mi
   H about 6 mi   J about 10 mi

9. **Write About It** Look back at the incorrect answer choices for Problem 5. Write each one as an amount of money.

_____

_____

Comparing and Ordering

Write the correct answer.

1. Write $>$, $<$, or $=$ to compare the two decimals.

    0.33 ◯ 0.3

    _____

2. Order the decimals 0.71, 0.81, 0.73, 0.8, and 0.7 from least to greatest. Use the number line.

    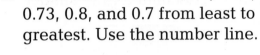

    0.7　　　0.8　　　0.9　　　1.0

    _____

3. Of the 10 members of Justin's soccer team, 6 played last year. Write a fraction and a decimal for the part of Justin's soccer team that played last year.

    _____

4. Krista spends $3\frac{1}{4}$ hours building a wall unit out of oak and another $4\frac{3}{4}$ hours applying finish to it. How many hours does she spend on the wall unit altogether?

    _____

Choose the letter of the correct answer.

5. Which decimal is the greatest number?

    A 0.2　　　　　**B** 0.02
    C 0.22　　　　**D** 0.20

6. Which group of decimals is ordered from the greatest to the least?

    F 0.38, 0.49, 0.4, 0.39
    G 0.35, 0.4, 0.41, 0.44
    H 0.22, 0.38, 0.3, 0.4
    J 0.41, 0.4, 0.38, 0.3

7. The Morrel family needs 32 square yards of carpeting for the family room. The length of the rectangular room is 24 feet. What is the width of the room?

    A 4 yd　　　　**B** 2 yd
    C 6 yd　　　　**D** Not Here

8. Jeremy's calculator has a random number function. When he presses the button, the calculator displays a random decimal between 0 and 1. He presses it four times. Which decimal is least?

    F 0.28　　　　**G** 0.3
    H 0.2　　　　**J** 0.25

9. **Write About It** Describe the steps you took to solve Problem 7.

    _____

    _____

Name _____

Mixed Decimals

Write the correct answer.

1. Write a mixed decimal for the model.

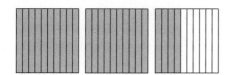

_____

2. Write a mixed decimal for the model.

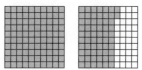

_____

3. Carol's recipe for modeling clay calls for $1\frac{3}{4}$ cups flour and $1\frac{1}{4}$ cups salt. Which ingredient does the recipe call for more of?

_____

4. The distance from Al's school to soccer practice is $2\frac{1}{4}$ miles. The distance from soccer practice home is $1\frac{3}{4}$ miles. If Al walks from school to soccer practice and then home, how far does he walk?

_____

Choose the letter of the correct answer.

5. Which mixed decimal is equivalent to $3\frac{3}{10}$?

   A 3.03   B 3.3

   C 0.33   D 3.33

6. Which mixed number is equivalent to 16.11?

   F $16\frac{1}{10}$ G $16\frac{11}{10}$

   H $16\frac{11}{1,000}$ J $16\frac{11}{100}$

7. Jan is building a model trestle bridge. He measures from one end of the bridge to drill holes for the supports. Here are the lengths he measures: $1\frac{3}{4}$ in., $4\frac{1}{4}$ in., $6\frac{3}{4}$ in., $9\frac{1}{4}$ in., $11\frac{3}{4}$ in. Continue the pattern to decide where he should mark the hole for the sixth support.

   A $14\frac{3}{4}$ in.   B $13\frac{3}{4}$ in.

   C $14\frac{1}{4}$ in.   D $12\frac{3}{4}$ in.

8. Kit has a digital stopwatch that counts seconds. He turns it on at 40 seconds after 12:58 P.M. He turns it off at 10 seconds after 1:09 P.M. How many seconds have passed?

   F 630 sec   G 750 sec

   H 670 sec   J Not Here

9. **Write About It** Write a rule for the pattern you used to solve Problem 7.

_____

_____

Word Clues

Word clues are the key words or phrases that help you understand what you need to do to solve a problem. Phrases like "the greatest," "the least," and "in order" are examples of word clues. Read the following problem.

VOCABULARY
word clues

> Mira rode 3 tests at the horse contest. She scored 59.32 on Test A, 61.50 on Test B, and 59.24 on Test C. List the tests in order from highest score to lowest score. Which was Mira's best test?

1. Underline the word clues to help you understand what the problem is asking you to do. Then explain what those word clues tell you.

Word Clues	Explanation
List the tests in order from highest score to lowest score.	
Which was Mira's best test?	

2. Solve the problem. _____

3. Describe the strategy you used. _____

Underline the word clues that help you solve each problem.
Solve.

4. The three riders with the highest scores will advance to the finals. Joel scored 59.82, Lori scored 60.93, Tanya scored 61.54, Dave scored 58.75, Sue scored 58.59, and Wayne scored 59.33. Who will advance to the finals?

_____

_____

5. The three riders with the highest average scores at the end of the year will be awarded trophies. Stephanie's average score is 59.67, Renee's is 61.20, Doug's is 58.04, Karen's is 60.18, Julio's is 60.56, and Katya's is 62.12. Who will be awarded the year-end trophies?

_____

_____

Adding Decimals

Write the correct answer.

1. Solve.

$$0.8 \\ + 0.5$$

_____

2. Solve.

$$1.83 \\ + 0.58$$

_____

3. Natasha has a handful of pennies. She counts 28 pennies. What decimal part of a dollar does she have?

_____

4. Mr. Moore fills the gasoline tank in his car. He then uses $\frac{1}{4}$ of the gasoline driving to his brother's house. How much of the tank of gasoline does he have left?

_____

Choose the letter of the correct answer.

5.

$$2.75 \\ + 1.35$$

A 3.00 **B** 3.10 **C** 4.00 **D** 4.10

6.

$$0.9 \\ + 0.7$$

F 1.6 **G** 1.16 **H** 1.66 **J** 0.16

7. A composer writes a symphony in 4 parts. Each part is twice as long as the previous part. The second part lasts for 6 minutes. How long is the entire symphony?

A 45 min   **B** 90 min
C 75 min   **D** 24 min

8. Mike spends $10.90 on dinner and $7.50 on a movie. He then spends $\frac{1}{2}$ of what he has left on a cab ride home. When he gets home he has $10.80 left. How much did Mike spend on the cab ride home?

F $40.00   **G** $60.00
H $10.80   **J** Not Here

9. Write About It Describe the method you used to solve Problem 7.

_____

_____

_____

_____

Subtracting Decimals

Write the correct answer.

1. Solve.

$$
\begin{array}{r}
0.8 \\
- 0.5 \\
\hline
\end{array}
$$

_____

2. Solve.

$$
\begin{array}{r}
1.23 \\
- 0.48 \\
\hline
\end{array}
$$

_____

3. Hank catches the flu, and his temperature rises to 3.2°F above normal. If normal is 98.6°F, what is Hank's temperature?

_____

4. Jenny cuts 3 lengths of molding: $3\frac{3}{4}$ inches, $3\frac{3}{8}$ inches, and $3\frac{3}{16}$ inches. Which is the shortest length she cuts?

_____

Choose the letter of the correct answer.

5.
$$
\begin{array}{r}
2.4 \\
- 1.5 \\
\hline
\end{array}
$$

A 0.09 **B** 0.99 **C** 1.9 **D** 0.9

6.
$$
\begin{array}{r}
0.57 \\
- 0.39 \\
\hline
\end{array}
$$

F 1.8 **G** 0.18 **H** 0.018 **J** 1.18

7. Long-playing vinyl records were usually meant to be played at a speed of $33\frac{1}{3}$ revolutions per minute. At this rate of speed, how many turns would it make in 3 minutes?

A Less than 100
B Exactly 100
C More than 100
D Not Here

8. At the start of the track season, Alicia's time in the 100-meter dash was 12.25 seconds. By the end of the season, her time dropped to 11.78 seconds. Which most accurately describes how Alicia's time improved?

F It fell almost 0.5 sec.
G It fell more than 0.5 sec.
H It fell almost 0.75 sec.
J It fell more than 0.75 sec.

9. Write About It Describe the steps you took to solve Problem 7.

_____

_____

Using Decimals

Write the correct answer.

1. Solve.

$$\begin{array}{r} 2.95 \\ +\ 3.77 \\ \hline \end{array}$$

_____

2. Solve.

$$\begin{array}{r} 7.08 \\ -\ 3.44 \\ \hline \end{array}$$

_____

3. Kate prices turquoise beads at four stores. She finds these prices for single beads: $0.98, $0.88, $0.95, $0.93. Order the prices from least to most expensive.

_____

4. Victor works $5\frac{1}{4}$ hours on Friday and $7\frac{3}{4}$ hours on Saturday. How much longer does he work on Saturday than on Friday?

_____

Choose the letter of the correct answer.

5.

$$\begin{array}{r} 8.42 \\ -\ 2.05 \\ \hline \end{array}$$

A 6.37   **B** 10.47

C 6.40   **D** 6.27

6.

$$\begin{array}{r} 0.07 \\ +\ 9.98 \\ \hline \end{array}$$

F 10.5   **G** 9.91

H 10.68   **J** 10.05

7. Two standard settings for laser printers are 300 dots per inch and 600 dots per inch. At 300 dots per inch, the printer will make 300 rows of dots along each inch of paper. How many more dots are there in 1 square inch printed at 600 dots per inch than in 1 square inch printed at 300 dots per inch?

A 2 times as many

B 3 times as many

C 4 times as many

D Not Here

8. Leanne buys a bookshelf that has the lowest shelf $3\frac{2}{4}$ in. above the floor. The next shelf up is $12\frac{3}{4}$ in. above the floor. Which of the following books will stand up straight on the lowest shelf?

F a $9\frac{1}{2}$-in.-tall book

G a $9\frac{3}{4}$-in.-tall book

H a $9\frac{5}{8}$-in.-tall book

J a $9\frac{1}{4}$-in.-tall book

9. Write About It Describe the strategy you used to solve Problem 7.

_____

_____

_____

Determine When to Estimate

It is often helpful to estimate the answer to a problem. Estimating can help you tell whether your solution is reasonable. One way to estimate is front-end estimation. Keep the first digit in each number as is, and change all the other digits to zero. Read the following problem.

> Julie ran 1.75 miles on Monday, 2.25 miles on Wednesday, and 3.3 miles on Friday. About how many miles did she run on those three days?

1. Estimate the answer. Keep the first digit in each number as is, and change the other digits to zero.

approximate miles run on Monday	approximate miles run on Wednesday	approximate miles run on Friday	total miles run on three days	Add to find total.
_____ + _____ + _____ = _____				
Since you changed each number to a lesser number, the estimated answer of _____ is less than the exact answer.				

2. Solve the problem. Explain what the estimate tells you.

_____

3. Describe the strategy you used. _____

_____

Estimate the answer. Explain what the estimate tells you.

4. Larry bought his lunch on three days this past week. He spent $5.84 on Tuesday, $4.30 on Wednesday, and $5.05 on Thursday. About how much did he spend on the three days?

5. Joelle scored 9.20 in the first ice-skating event. She scored 8.45 in the second event and 9.61 in the third event. About how many points did she score in all?

Name _____

Estimating Sums and Differences by Rounding

Write the correct answer.

1. Estimate the sum by rounding to the nearest whole number.

$$
\begin{array}{r}
2.4 \\
1.8 \\
+\ 3.7 \\
\hline
\end{array}
$$

_____

2. Estimate the difference by rounding to the nearest whole number.

$$
\begin{array}{r}
6.7 \\
-\ 2.3 \\
\hline
\end{array}
$$

_____

3. Chuck and Phyllis want to buy a $1.39 mouse pad. Chuck has $0.85 and Phyllis has $0.48. Together, do they have enough for the mouse pad?

_____

4. A chemist has a beaker with 2.8 liters of alcohol in it. She pours 1.6 liters of it into a flask. How much alcohol is left in the beaker?

_____

Choose the letter of the correct answer.

5. Which is the most reasonable estimate of the sum?

$$
\begin{array}{r}
1.72 \\
+\ 1.63 \\
\hline
\end{array}
$$

  A 3.3   **B** 3
  C 4.3   **D** 0.1

6. Which is the most reasonable estimate of the difference?

$$
\begin{array}{r}
7.58 \\
-\ 2.81 \\
\hline
\end{array}
$$

  F 4   **G** 4.8
  H 10   **J** 5.8

7. A song is played at a fast tempo of 150 beats per minute. If the song lasts for 3 minutes 40 seconds, about how many beats are there in the song?

  A 400 beats
  B 300 beats
  C 500 beats
  D 600 beats

8. A pixel is an individual dot. Some computer monitors are 1,024 pixels wide by 768 pixels high. About how many pixels are there on such a computer screen?

  F about 80,000
  G about 800,000
  H about 1,800
  J about 8,000

9. **Write About It** Describe the steps you took to solve Problem 7.

_____

_____

_____

Linear Measures

Write the correct answer.

1. Choose the most reasonable unit to use to measure the distance from your town to the state line. Write *in.*, *ft*, *yd*, or *mi.*

   _____

2. Choose the most reasonable unit to use to measure the length of a chalkboard in your classroom. Write *in.*, *ft*, *yd*, or *mi.*

   _____

3. Write the most reasonable unit to use to measure the distance a football player carries the ball down the field: *in.*, *ft*, *yd*, or *mi.*

   _____

4. Write the most reasonable unit for a tailor to use to measure the length of a jacket sleeve: *in.*, *ft*, *yd*, or *mi.*

   _____

Choose the letter of the correct answer.

5. Which is the longest measurement?

   A 22 in.   **B** 22 mi
   C 22 ft   **D** 22 yd

6. Which unit would be the most reasonable one to use to measure the amount of rain that falls in one month?

   F in.   **G** ft   **H** yd   **J** mi

7. A course of bricks is one layer of bricks in a wall. If each brick is $2\frac{1}{2}$ inches high and there is $\frac{1}{2}$ inch. of mortar between courses, how many courses will be needed in a wall that must be at least 40 inches high?

   A 16 courses   **B** 10 courses
   C 14 courses   **D** 15 courses

8. A square pasture is surrounded by 12,000 feet of fencing. Which operation can you use to find the length of each side?

   F addition
   G subtraction
   H multiplication
   J division

9. **Write About It** Explain your solution to Problem 7.

   _____

   _____

   _____

Changing Units

Write the correct answer.

1. Write the measure using the new unit.

   48 in. = _____ ft

2. Write the measure using the new unit.

   2 mi = _____ ft

3. Jocelyn wants to measure the size of her computer screen. Which unit of measure should she use?

   _____

4. Brad wants to measure the length of his pickup truck. Which unit of measure should he use?

   _____

Choose the letter of the correct answer.

5. Which word makes the sentence true?

   To change from yd to mi, you __?__.

   A add   B subtract
   C multiply   D divide

6. Which measurement is equivalent to 360 in.?

   F 36 ft   G 30 yd
   H 10 yd   J 100 yd

7. The distance from Earth to the Moon is about 250,000 miles. The distance from Earth to the Sun is about 400 times the distance from Earth to the Moon. Estimate the distance from Earth to the Sun.

   A About 250,000,000 mi
   B About 150,000,000 mi
   C About 100,000 mi
   D About 100,000,000 mi

8. Tom writes the digits 0–9 on 10 pieces of paper, folds the pieces of paper, and puts them all in a hat. He picks a piece of paper without looking. For which of the numbers below is the probability $\frac{1}{10}$?

   F 3
   G 7
   H 9
   J Not Here

9. **Write About It** Explain the steps you took to solve Problem 7.

   _____

   _____

Sequencing

Sequence is an arrangement of one thing after another. You can use sequence clues to determine the order of events in a problem. Look for words such as *first*, *last*, *next*, *then*, *now*, *before*, *after*, and *already*. Read the following problem.

> Henry made a coatrack from a board. He placed the first peg 4 in. from the left end. He placed the last peg 4 in. from the right end. He also placed 1 peg every 4 in. between the end pegs. The board he used was already cut to 3 ft long. How many pegs did he use?

1. Underline the sequence clues below. Then list each event in the order in which it happened.

Sequence Clues	Order of Events
He placed the first peg 4 in. from the left end.	
He placed the last peg 4 in. from the right end.	
He placed 1 peg every 4 in.	
The board he used was already cut to 3 ft.	

2. Solve the problem. _____

3. Describe the strategy you used. _____

Underline the sequence clues in each problem. Solve.

4. Lenore hung paintings on one wall in the art gallery. After she measured the wall to be 8 yd, she hung the first picture 6 ft from the left end of the wall. Then she hung 1 painting every 6 ft. The last thing she did was hang a painting 6 ft from the right end of the wall. How many paintings did Lenore hang?

5. Howard made a long banner with flags from different countries. After cutting out a 4-ft-long piece of cloth for the banner, he glued the first flag 6 in. from the left end. Next he glued 1 flag every 6 in. He glued the last flag 6 in. from the right end. How many flags did Howard glue onto the banner?

Name _____

Fractions in Measurement

Write the correct answer.

1. Measure the length of the screw to the nearest $\frac{1}{2}$ inch.

_____

2. Measure the length of the clip to the nearest $\frac{1}{4}$ inch.

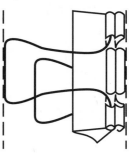

_____

3. William measures the height of his 2-year-old brother to see how much he has grown. Which unit of measure should he use?

_____

4. An award-winning running back has carried the football for a total of 1,760 yards this season. How many miles is this?

_____

Choose the letter of the correct answer.

5. Which is the measure of the screw in Problem 1 to the nearest $\frac{1}{4}$ in.?

   A 1 in.   **B** $1\frac{1}{4}$ in.

   C $1\frac{2}{4}$ in.   **D** $1\frac{3}{4}$ in.

6. Which is the measure of the clip in Problem 2 to the nearest $\frac{1}{2}$ in.?

   F 1 in.   **G** $1\frac{1}{2}$ in.

   H 2 in.   **J** $2\frac{1}{2}$ in.

7. If February 29 falls on a Friday in one year, which day of the week will April 1 fall on in that year?

   A Monday   **B** Tuesday
   C Wednesday   **D** Thursday

8. Henry measured a length of wood as 7 inches to the nearest inch. Which of the following lengths could *not* be the one Henry measured?

   F $6\frac{3}{4}$ in.   **G** $7\frac{3}{8}$ in.

   H $7\frac{5}{8}$ in.   **J** Not Here

9. **Write About It** What are the longest and the shortest lengths that could be labeled "7 inches to the nearest inch"?

_____

_____

Weight

Write the correct answer.

1. Choose the most reasonable unit to measure the weight of the item. Write *oz*, *lb*, or *T*.

_____

2. Choose the most reasonable unit to measure the weight of the item. Write *oz*, *lb*, or *T*.

_____

3. Dave needs 4 cups of whipping cream for a pie. The store sells whipping cream in 1-pint containers. How many pints should Dave buy?

_____

4. Lucy needs to fill up a large wash tub so she can give her Great Dane a bath. She wants to know the capacity of the wash tub. What unit of measure should she use?

_____

Choose the letter of the correct answer.

5. Which measurement is equivalent to 3 tons?

   A 2,000 lb   B 6,000 lb
   C 600 lb   D 6,000 oz

6. Which measurement is equivalent to 64 ounces?

   F 2 lb   G 4 lb   H 6 lb   J 8 lb

7. Chas has 6 coins in his pocket. Which amount could *not* be the total value of his 6 coins?

   A $0.15
   B $1.50
   C $0.20
   D $0.10

8. A riddle asks, "Which weighs more: a ton of bricks, or a ton of feathers?" Suppose a brick weighs 1 lb. Together 20 feathers weigh about 1 oz. About how many more feathers than bricks would you need to have 1 T?

   F About 320 times as many
   G About 160 times as many
   H About 1,600 times as many
   J Not Here

9. **Write About It** Describe the method you used to solve Problem 8.

_____

_____

Name _____

LESSON
25.1

Linear Measures

Write the correct answer.

1. Choose the most reasonable unit to use to measure the length of a baseball field. Write *cm, dm,* or *m.*

   _____

2. Choose the most reasonable unit to use to measure the width of a computer disk. Write *cm, dm,* or *m.*

   _____

3. Ty says that his new baby sister weighs 128 ounces. Write his sister's weight in pounds.

   _____

4. Melanie is 48 inches tall. Write Melanie's height using feet.

   _____

Choose the letter of the correct answer.

5. Which measurement is equivalent to 1 meter?

   A 100 dm   **B** 10 cm
   C 100 cm   **D** 1,000 dm

6. Which measurement is equivalent to 15,840 feet?

   F 2 mi   **G** 3,520 yd
   H 3 mi   **J** 1,760 yd

7. These are the heights of the 5 starting players on the basketball team: 73 inches, 76 inches, 64 inches, 69 inches, 78 inches What is the team's average height in feet?

   A 5 ft   **B** $5\frac{1}{2}$ ft

   C 6 ft   **D** $6\frac{1}{2}$ ft

8. A book with 28 chapters has an average of 16 pages per chapter. The book also has a foreword of 12 pages and an index of 8 pages. Which expression could you use to find the total number of pages in the book?

   F $28 \times (16 + 12 + 8)$
   G $28 \times (16 + 8) + 12$
   H $(28 \times 16) + 12 + 8$
   J Not Here

9. **Write About It** Describe how you decided whether to multiply or divide Problems 3 and 4.

   _____

   _____

   _____

   _____

PROBLEM SOLVING   PS127

Decimals and Metric Measures

Write the correct answer.

1. Write the missing metric unit of measure.

$$120 \text{ cm} = \underline{\hspace{2cm}} \text{ m}$$

2. Write the missing metric unit of measure.

$$40 \text{ dm} = \underline{\hspace{2cm}} \text{ m}$$

3. Coach McHugh is marking off the sidelines for a soccer field. Which unit of measure would be most reasonable, *cm, dm,* or *m*?

4. There are 8 children in the Caitlin household. If each of the children drinks 1 cup of milk with dinner, how many quarts of milk do they drink altogether at dinner time?

Choose the letter of the correct answer.

5. Which number makes the measures equivalent?

$$60 \text{ cm} = \underline{\overset{?}{\hspace{0.5cm}}} \text{ m}$$

   A 0.06   **B** 0.6   **C** 6.0   **D** 6,000

6. Which number makes the measures equivalent?

$$20 \text{ dm} = \underline{\overset{?}{\hspace{0.5cm}}} \text{ m}$$

   F 2   **G** 0.2   **H** 200   **J** 2,000

7. On Saturday, Taylor bowled three games. His scores were 121, 133, and 112. What was Taylor's average bowling score on Saturday?

   A 114
   B 118
   C 122
   D 127

8. The early train to Nattick leaves Dexter station at 5:55 A.M. The last train to Nattick leaves Dexter station at 11:15 P.M. How much time elapses between the departure of the last train and the departure of the early train the next morning?

   F 17 hr 20 min   **G** 17 hr 40 min
   H 6 hr 40 min   **J** Not Here

9. **Write About It** Explain the method you used to solve Problem 8.

_____

_____

_____

Name _____

Changing Units

Write the correct answer.

1. Write the number you would multiply by to change meters to decimeters.

$$m = \underline{\ ?\ } \times dm$$

_____

2. Write the number in the blank to make the measures equivalent.

$$18\ dm = \underline{\ ?\ }\ cm$$

_____

3. Sonia is 132 centimeters tall. How many meters tall is she?

_____

4. Diane knows her family's pickup truck can carry a load of as much as 2 tons. How many pounds is this?

_____

Choose the letter of the correct answer.

5. Which measure is equivalent to 37 decimeters?

   A 3.7 cm   B 370 cm
   C 370 m   D 3,700 cm

6. Which measure is equivalent to 420 meters?

   F 42 dm   G 4,200 cm
   H 42,000 cm   J 420 dm

7. The temperature at 6:00 A.M. is 32°F. By 10:00 A.M., it has risen to 44°F. By noon, it has risen another 3°F. It then begins to fall. At 3:00 P.M., it is 6°F below its noontime high. At sundown, it is 30°F. How much did the temperature fall between 3:00 P.M. and sundown?

   A 11°F   B 14°F
   C 41°F   D 44°F

8. Jon has scores of 88, 92, 81, 98, and 86 on his math tests. What is Jon's average score?

   F 98   G 95
   H 89   J Not Here

9. **Write About It** Describe the steps you took to solve Problem 8.

_____

_____

Making Inferences

To **make inferences** means to draw conclusions based on the given information. In order to make an inference, you must examine all of the given information. Read the following problem.

VOCABULARY
make
    inferences

> In the morning, Mary and Billy each caught one fish. Mary's fish measured 9 decimeters and Billy's fish measured 1.1 meters. In the afternoon, Mary caught another fish. Mary caught the longest fish of the day. What inference can you make about the fish that Mary caught in the afternoon?

1. Examine the information given in the problem. Then make inferences about that information.

Information	Inference
Length of Mary's first fish is _____. Length of Billy's fish is _____. Length of Mary's second fish is unknown. Mary caught the longest fish.	
Mary's first fish is _____ cm long. Billy's fish is _____ cm long.	

2. Solve the problem. _____

_____

3. Describe the strategy you used. _____

Make inferences to solve.

4. Tony and Tomiko raced toy cars. In the first trial, Tony's car went 18 decimeters and Tomiko's car went 1.7 meters. In the second trial, Tony's car went 17 decimeters and Tomiko's car went the longest distance out of the two trials. What inference can you make about the second trial?_____

_____

Capacity

Write the correct answer.

1. Choose the most reasonable unit for measuring the capacity of a coffee mug. Write *mL, metric cup,* or *L.*

_____

2. Choose the most reasonable unit for measuring the capacity of a bottle of water. Write *mL, metric cup,* or *L.*

_____

3. Joy estimates that her dripping bathtub faucet would take only 1 week to fill the bathtub. She wants to estimate how much water that is. Which unit of capacity should she use: cup, quart, or gallon?

_____

4. Brian is school champ at the 100-meter dash. He wants to know how many centimeters are in 100 meters. Find the answer.

_____

Choose the letter of the correct answer.

5. What is the most reasonable measurement for the capacity of a goldfish bowl?

A 2 L   **B** 20 L
C 200 mL   **D** 20 mL

6. What is the most reasonable measurement for the capacity of a car's gasoline tank?

F 4 L   **G** 40 L
H 40 mL   **J** 400 mL

7. Brennan opens a bottle of apple juice and drinks 8 oz of it. He pours the same amount into a pot of applesauce he is making. His sister then drinks 4 oz of the juice and pours a 4-oz glass for their mother. Brennan and his father each drink a 4-oz. glass. How many ounces of juice were in the bottle when Brennan opened it?

A 32 oz   **B** 40 oz
C 96 oz   **D** 128 oz

8. What is the next number in the pattern?

12, 24, 36, 48, 60, 72, _?_

F 68   **G** 74
H 192   **J** Not Here

9. **Write About It** Describe the strategy you used to solve Problem 7.

_____

_____

_____

Time as a Fraction

Write the correct answer.

1. Write a word name using *a quarter* or *half* for the time shown.

_____

2. Write a word name using *a quarter* or *half* for the time shown.

_____

3. Mr. Nesbitt, the math teacher, tells his class he was on the track team in college. He tells them he ran the 40,000 cm race. Write this distance using meters to find the common name of this event.

_____

4. Andrea is buying spices to use in her spice cookies. Should she expect to buy the spices by the gram or by the kilogram?

_____

Choose the letter of the correct answer.

5. Which time is another way of writing "half past eleven"?

A 11:15   **B** 11:45
C 10:30   **D** 11:30

6. Which phrase is another way of saying the time 3:45?

F a quarter past four
G a quarter to three
H a quarter past three
J a quarter to four

7. In Britain, it is common to say "half ten" for what Americans would call "half past ten." Which time would some British people call "half twelve"?

A 11:30   **B** 12:30
C 12:45   **D** Not Here

8. A desktop printer is supposed to print $4\frac{1}{2}$ pages per minute. If you leave the printer running for an hour, about how many pages could you expect to have printed?

F About 90 pages
G About 120 pages
H About 150 pages
J About 270 pages

9. Write About It Explain how you estimated the answer to Problem 8.

_____

_____

Choosing Customary or Metric Units

Write the correct answer.

1. Write the more reasonable
   measurement for the paper clip:
   3 centimeters or 3 inches.

   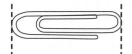

   _____

2. Write the more reasonable
   measurement for the flower:
   2 centimeters or 2 inches.

   _____

3. Ed is supposed to meet his sister at
   school at a quarter to three. He
   arrives at 3:15. Is he on time?

   _____

4. The width of Ophelia's desk is
   220 centimeters. Is her desk wider
   than 2 meters?

   _____

Choose the letter of the correct answer.

5. Wendy catches the school bus at
   half past seven every morning. The
   bus drops her off at school at a
   quarter after eight. Which shows the
   amount of time her bus trip takes?

   A 30 min   **B** 45 min
   C 15 min   **D** 1 hr 15 min

6. A catalog lists the height of a desk
   as "30," but the page is torn and
   the unit of measure is missing.
   Which is the most reasonable unit
   to go after the "30"?

   F cm   **G** in.   **H** ft   **J** m

7. The fourth-grade students at North
   Country Elementary collected 90
   aluminum cans of food each week.
   After 8 weeks, they delivered their
   cans to the Food Bank. How many
   cans did they deliver?

   A 360 cans   **B** 450 cans
   C 540 cans   **D** 720 cans

8. If a measure of 10 in. is about
   equal to a measure of 25 cm,
   which of these measures is about
   equal to a measure of 100 in.?

   F 250 cm   **G** 2,500 cm
   H 500 cm   **J** Not Here

9. **Write About It** What method did you use to solve Problem 5?

   _____

   _____

Understanding Multistep Problems

Sometimes you need to take more than one step to solve a problem. It is important to read the problem carefully first and to consider all the given facts. Read the following problem.

> There were 48 people at the photography club banquet. They were divided into 4 equal groups. Three of the groups sat at round tables. How many people sat at round tables?

1. Read the problem carefully. List the given facts. Solve the problem one step at a time. Match the facts to number sentences.

Facts	Steps
There were_____ people. They were divided into_____equal groups.	1.
_____ groups sat at round tables.	2.

2. Solve the problem. _____

3. Describe the strategy you used._____

_____

Solve each problem one step at a time. Write a number sentence for each step.

4. Donna is placing stones around a fish pool. The pool is a rectangle 6 feet long and 3 feet wide. What is the perimeter of the pool in yards?

_____

_____

5. Zeke buys 3 tickets to the fair. Each costs $7.50. He has a coupon for $1.50 off one ticket. How much does he pay for all 3 tickets?

_____

_____

6. There are 41 students on each of 3 buses. On a mini-bus, there are 12 more students. How many students are there on all the buses?

_____

_____

7. Babs works from 8:15 A.M. to 12:15 P.M. and from 1:30 p.m. to 6:00 P.M. How long does Babs work?

_____

_____

Temperature

Write the correct answer.

1. The thermometer shows the water temperature in °F. The air temperature is 78°F. What is the difference between the two temperatures?

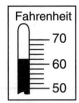

2. The thermometer shows the noon temperature in °C. The midnight temperature was 6°C. How many degrees did the temperature rise between midnight and noon?

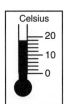

3. Nora finds a package of computer paper that is marked width: 21.5. Which is the more likely unit of measure—centimeters or inches?

4. Jonathan weighs each letter to find the postage needed for mailing. Which unit of measure would he probably use—ounces or pounds?

Choose the letter of the correct answer.

5. Which choice shows the difference between the temperatures 10°F and ‾20°F?

   A 10°F   B 30°F
   C 20°F   D 40°F

6. Which choice shows how much time elapses between half past noon and quarter to one?

   F 30 min   G 15 min
   H 45 min   J 1 hr 15 min

7. Which time comes next in this pattern? quarter to noon, half past one, quarter past three, five o'clock, __?__

   A half past six
   B quarter to six
   C quarter past six
   D quarter to seven

8. Joan has 2 ft of ribbon to make a frame around a photograph. Which of these photos would the ribbon fit around with none left over?

   F a 3-in. by 5-in. photo
   G a 4-in. by 6-in. photo
   H a 2-in. by 3-in. photo
   J a 5-in. by 7-in. photo

9. **Write About It** Describe the method you used to solve Problem 7.

_____

_____

_____

Using Division Patterns to Estimate

Write the correct answer.

1. Round the divisor and the dividend. Estimate the quotient.

   446 ÷ 93

   _____

2. Round the divisor and the dividend. Estimate the quotient.

   652 ÷ 77

   _____

3. Write the basic fact you can use to help you estimate the quotient.

   535 ÷ 58

   _____

4. Write the basic fact you can use to help you estimate the quotient.

   267 ÷ 31

   _____

Choose the letter of the correct answer.

5. Which number will finish the pattern?

   $$90 \div 30 = 3$$
   $$900 \div 30 = 30$$
   $$9,000 \div 30 = 300$$
   $$90,000 \div 30 = \underline{\ ?\ }$$

   A 30,000   **B** 3,000
   C 30   **D** 300

6. Which number will finish the pattern?

   $$80 \div 40 = 2$$
   $$800 \div 40 = 20$$
   $$8,000 \div 40 = 200$$
   $$\underline{\ ?\ } \div 40 = 2,000$$

   F 800   **G** 800,000
   H 8,000   **J** 80,000

7. Ms. Felton makes $22 an hour as a consultant. How much did she earn during the week of January 19, 1998?

   Hours Worked Week of Jan. 19, 1998

Day	Mon	Tue	Wed	Thu	Fri	Sat
Time	6 hr	8 hr	10 hr	9 hr	5 hr	6 hr

   A $898   **B** $360
   C $880   **D** $968

8. A theater company rents a stage for a total of 32 hours. They pay $296 for the space. Which is the most reasonable estimate of what they pay for the space each hour?

   F $18   **G** $6
   H $10   **J** $12

9. **Write About It** Describe the pattern of zeros you used to help you find the missing number in Problems 5 and 6.

   _____

   _____

Dividing by Tens

Write the correct answer.

1. Write the number of digits there will be in the quotient.

$40\overline{)960}$

_____

2. Solve.

$60\overline{)792}$

_____

3. Amanda is packing oranges at her parents' produce stand. Each box holds 18 oranges. A load of about 150 oranges is delivered. About how many boxes will Amanda need to hold all the oranges?

_____

4. At the Campanella School, 475 students are going on the field trip to Rockefeller Center. Each bus can carry 62 students. How many buses are needed?

_____

Choose the letter of the correct answer.

5. $30\overline{)383}$

A 12 r13   B 12 r23
C 13 r13   D 12

6. $50\overline{)776}$

F 31 r1   G 15 r1
H 75 r1   J 15 r26

7. An Internet service provider runs 37 servers. Each server gets about 30,000 visits, or "hits," each day. Which of the following is the most reasonable claim for the service provider to make?

A More than 500 hits a day!
B More than 1 million hits a day!
C More than 2 million hits a day!
D More than 5 million hits a day!

8. Iris turns 10 years old today. Which is the most reasonable estimate for the number of minutes Iris has been alive?

F 50,000   G 500,000
H 5,000,000   K Not Here

9. **Write About It** Explain how you chose your estimate in Problem 8.

_____

_____

_____

Division Procedures

Write the correct answer.

1. $34\overline{)578}$

2. $52\overline{)921}$

_____

3. Gerry runs probability experiments on his computer. Each experiment takes 20 days complete. What is the greatest number of experiments he can run in 1 year (365 days)?

4. Lee completes a 930-mile car trip at an average speed of about 60 miles per hour. About how many hours did she spend driving on the trip?

Choose the letter of the correct answer.

5. $28\overline{)656}$

   A 22 r16   B 23 r12
   C 22 r18   D 23 r2

6. $47\overline{)781}$

   F 12 r15   G 18 r2
   H 17 r31   J 16 r29

7. Tina finds this fraction pattern in an old math book: $\frac{3}{4}, \frac{3}{8}, \frac{4}{8}, \frac{4}{16}, \frac{5}{16}, \frac{5}{32}.$ Which is the next fraction in the pattern?

   A $\frac{6}{64}$

   B $\frac{5}{64}$

   C $\frac{6}{32}$

   D $\frac{6}{16}$

8. Felicia flips a nickel 30 times and records how it lands, heads up or tails up. She records 16 heads and 14 tails. Which of the following is reasonable for her to conclude?

   F If you toss a coin 30 times, you will always toss 14 tails.
   G The probability of tossing heads is greater than that of tossing tails.
   H The probability of tossing heads or tails is about $\frac{1}{2}$.
   J If you toss a coin 30 times, you will always get 16 heads.

9. **Write About It** Describe the rule for the pattern you saw in Problem 7.

_____

_____

Drawing Conclusions

Drawing conclusions is an important part of solving problems. To draw conclusions, you must examine the information in the problem and use what you already know to find the answer. Read the following problem.

VOCABULARY

drawing conclusions

Carol put a fence with a perimeter of 24 feet around her garden. Robert put a fence with a perimeter of 12 yards around his garden. Whose fence has the greater perimeter?

1. Under Examine the Information complete the information that is given in the problem. In the next column, write some helpful information that you already know. Use this information to help you draw a conclusion.

Examine the Information	Use What You Already Know
• The perimeter of Carol's garden is _____.	• There are _____ feet in 1 yard.
• The perimeter of Robert's garden is _____.	• To change feet to yards, _____.

Draw Conclusions

24 feet = _____ yards

2. Solve the problem. _____

3. Describe the strategy you used. _____

_____

Examine the information and use what you already know to draw conclusions. Solve.

4. On Friday, Pam's niece was just 18 months old. Peter's niece was exactly 64 weeks old. What is the age of Peter's niece in months? Whose niece is older?

_____

5. Jack worked in the yard for 2 hours. His brother, Jake, worked in the yard for 180 minutes. How many hours did Jake work? Who worked in the yard longer?

_____

Correcting Quotients

Write the correct answer.

1. Write *too high, too low,* or *just right* to describe the estimated quotient.

$$42\overline{)368}^{9}$$

_____

2. Write *too high, too low,* or *just right* to describe the estimated quotient.

$$77\overline{)231}^{2}$$

_____

3. The wrestling team spent $375 buying sweatshirts for its 25 wrestlers. How much did each sweatshirt cost?

_____

4. The administrator who manages the school computers orders 36 copies of a software package. The total charge will be $972. What is the cost for a single copy?

_____

Choose the letter of the correct answer.

5. $71\overline{)365}$

    A 4 r10   **B** 5 r10

    C 6 r10   **D** 4 r61

6. $58\overline{)447}$

    F 5 r33   **G** 6 r45

    H 8 r3   **J** 7 r41

7. Ben takes 7 rolls of the same coins to the bank. Which choice can *not* be the total value of the 7 coin rolls?

Coin	penny	nickel	dime	quarter
Number in roll	50	40	50	40

    A $3.50   **B** $7.00

    C $14.00   **D** $70.00

8. Brita has 372 dimes and 185 nickels. She puts the dimes in rolls of 50 per roll and the nickels in rolls of 40 per roll. How many rolls does she have?

    F 7 dime rolls, 3 nickel rolls

    G 6 dime rolls, 4 nickel rolls

    H 7 dime rolls, 4 nickel rolls

    J Not Here

9. **Write About It** Describe the steps you took to solve Problem 8.

_____

_____

Fractions in Circle Graphs

Write the correct answer.

1. What fraction of the students named baseball as their favorite sport?

_____

2. What fraction of the students in the circle graph in Problem 1 named basketball as their favorite sport?

_____

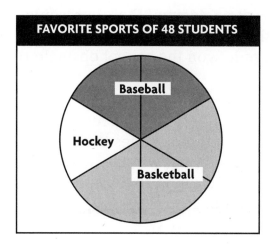

FAVORITE SPORTS OF 48 STUDENTS

Baseball

Hockey

Basketball

3. Carrie packs 30 doughnuts to a carton. How many full cartons can she pack from a batch of 250 doughnuts?

_____

4. Deb rents a rectangular apartment that is 992 sq ft. One wall measures 32 ft. What are the measures of the walls on either side?

_____

Choose the letter of the correct answer.

5. Which fraction represents the students in Problem 1 who named either hockey or basketball as their favorite sport?

   A $\frac{2}{6}$ **B** $\frac{1}{6}$ **C** $\frac{3}{6}$ **D** $\frac{4}{6}$

7. Earth takes 1,461 days to make 4 trips around the sun. How many days does it take the Earth to make 1 trip around the sun?

   A 30.25 days **B** 300 days
   C 365.25 days **D** 365 days

6. Which fraction represents all of the students surveyed for the circle graph in Problem 1?

   F $\frac{2}{6}$ **G** $\frac{4}{6}$ **H** $\frac{6}{6}$ **J** $\frac{7}{6}$

8. A bag holds 3 blue, 6 orange, and 4 red marbles. You pull a marble from the bag without looking. Which of the marbles do you have a $\frac{10}{13}$ probability of pulling?

   F an orange marble
   G a marble that is not white
   H an orange or a red marble
   J a red or a blue marble

9. **Write About It** Explain how you arrived at your answer to Problem 8.

_____

_____

Decimals in Circle Graphs

Write the correct answer.

1. Write a decimal that represents the number of times the fourth grade won the school obstacle run.

   _____

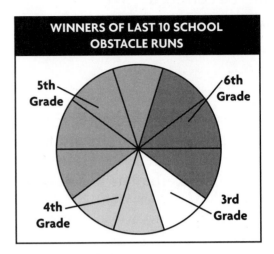

WINNERS OF LAST 10 SCHOOL OBSTACLE RUNS

5th Grade

6th Grade

4th Grade

3rd Grade

2. Write a decimal that represents the number of times the sixth grade did *not* win the school obstacle run in the graph in Problem 1.

   _____

3. Write a fraction that represents the number of times the third grade won the obstacle run in Problem 1.

   _____

4. A dozen eggs is 12 eggs. A *gross* of eggs is 144 eggs. How many dozen eggs are there in a gross?

   _____

Choose the letter of the correct answer.

5. Which decimal represents the total number of times the obstacle run is recorded in the circle graph in Problem 1?

   A 0.1   **B** 1.0   **C** 0.5   **D** 10

6. Which fraction represents the number of times the third or fourth grade won the obstacle run in the circle graph in Problem 1?

   F $\frac{1}{10}$ **G** $\frac{2}{10}$ **H** $\frac{3}{10}$ **J** $\frac{5}{10}$

7. Steve meets Janine for lunch at half past twelve. They have lunch for 45 minutes and then spend 30 minutes having a cup of coffee. What time is it when they leave?

   A quarter to two
   B quarter after two
   C half past two
   D quarter to three

8. The Borgers take an 880-mile car trip. They set out at 5:00 A.M., stop for lunch from 12:30 P.M. to 1:30 P.M., and stop for dinner from 5:00 P.M. to 6:30 P.M. They end their trip at 11:30 P.M. What is their average speed while they are driving?

   F 50 mi per hr   **G** 55 mi per hr
   H 60 mi per hr   **J** Not Here

9. **Write About It** Describe the steps you took to solve Problem 8.

   _____

   _____

Multiple-Meaning Words

Some problems contain words that have more than one
meaning. You can use information given in the problem to
determine which meaning of the word is being used. Read the
following problem.

> Mr. Wilson is building an *addition* to his house. The new
> room will have a length of 24 feet and a width of 18 feet.
> Use *addition* to find the perimeter of the new room.

1. Read the problem carefully to determine which word is used
   with more than one meaning. Write the word and the words
   around it. Write the meaning of the word each way it is
   being used.

Multiple-Meaning Word	Surrounding Phrase	Definition

2. Solve the problem. _____

3. Describe the strategy you used. _____

_____

Read the problem carefully to determine which word or words
might have multiple meanings. Underline the words. Solve.

4. Mr. Wilson will pound nails to build
   the wooden frame for his new room.
   He ordered 15 pounds of nails from
   a builder. Each pound of nails had
   about 150 nails. About how many
   nails does Mr. Wilson have in all?

5. The electric meter for the new
   room will be placed on the side of
   the house, 200 centimeters off the
   ground. How many meters high
   is this?

_____   _____

Name _____

Choosing Graphs to Represent Data

Write the correct answer.

1. Which graph shows that $\frac{1}{2}$ of the vehicles are cars?

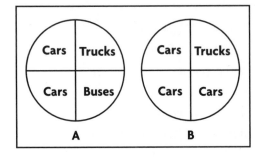

3. What fraction of the vehicles shown in Graph B above are cars?

_____

2. Which graph shows that $\frac{1}{4}$ of the vehicles are trucks?

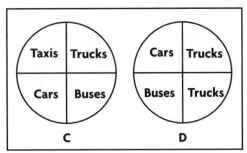

4. What fraction of the vehicles shown in Graph D above are either cars, trucks, or buses?

_____

Choose the letter of the correct answer.

5. Which graph in Problems 1 and 2 above shows that $\frac{1}{2}$ of the vehicles seen were trucks?

   A Graph A   B Graph B
   C Graph C   D Graph D

7. A circle graph is divided into 24 equal sections. The total number of people represented by the circle graph is 264. How many people are represented by each section?

   A 24 people   B 12 people
   C 10 people   D 11 people

6. Which fraction of the vehicles shown in Graph C in Problem 2 are *not* trucks?

   F $\frac{1}{4}$ G $\frac{2}{4}$ H $\frac{3}{4}$ J $\frac{4}{4}$

8. Christopher Columbus landed in Central America in 1492. George Washington was born 240 years later. Missouri became a state 89 years after that. In what year did Missouri become a state?

   F 1823   G 1818
   H 1821   J Not Here

9. **Write About It** Explain the method you used to solve Problem 7.

_____

_____